On Being Seen

On Being Seen
Chronicles of a Touch & Intimacy Therapist

By
R. Ayité Okyne

On Being Seen: Chronicles of a Touch & Intimacy Therapist

Copyright © 2024 by R. Ayité Okyne
All rights reserved.

No part of this book may be reproduced, stored in a retrieval system, or transmitted in any form or by any means—electronic, mechanical, photocopying, recording, or otherwise—without the prior written permission of the publisher, except in the case of brief quotations embodied in critical articles or reviews.

Publisher
Lifestyle Media Publishers

ISBN: 978-0-9899473-1-2
First Edition: January, 2025

This book is a work of creative nonfiction. The names used in this book are not the names of actual people. To protect the anonymity and privacy of my clients, all names and identifying details have been changed. The stories shared are based on real experiences but have been altered where necessary to ensure confidentiality. Any resemblance to actual persons, living or deceased, is purely coincidental.

Disclaimer
The information provided in this book is for educational and informational purposes only. This book is not a substitute for professional medical, psychological, or legal advice. If you have specific concerns or require assistance, please consult with a qualified professional. The author and publisher are not responsible for any outcomes resulting from the use of the information or resources provided in this book.

Printed in USA

For permissions or inquiries, please contact:
ayite@trevorjamesla.com

Cover photo by jpfotograaf.

DEDICATION

To my mother, Elsie, whose love has been my anchor and whose strength has been my guide.

To my siblings, Okailey, Ayikwei, and Leslie, my first circle of connection and inspiration, and the keepers of my laughter, my memories, and my heart.

And to my father, James, whose absence is felt as deeply as his presence once was—this book carries your legacy of kindness and connection.

For all that you've given me, and all that you've taught me about love, touch, and belonging—this is for you.

On Being Seen

HOW TO MAKE THE MOST OF THIS BOOK

This book is designed to meet you wherever you are on your journey. The chapters can be read in any order, allowing you to dive into the topics that feel most relevant to you right now. Whether you're curious about professional intimacy services, navigating emotional barriers, or exploring the role of touch in your life, each chapter stands alone as a resource for reflection and growth.

I encourage you to take your time. Pause to absorb the stories, revisit the chapters, and reflect on how the insights resonate with your own experiences. This is not a book you need to rush through—it's an invitation to explore, at your own pace, the power of connection, vulnerability, and being truly seen.

Above all, approach these pages with an open heart. Whether you read every word or just the sections that call to you, my hope is that this book offers you inspiration, validation, and practical tools to bring more connection into your life.

TABLE OF CONTENTS

Prologue	1
My Personal Struggle with Touch and Intimacy	5
A Hand to Hold	11
Why This Book Matters	15
Part 1: The Silent Struggles of Men	**21**
Chapter 1: A Culture of Disconnection	23
Chapter 2: Touch Hunger in Men	33
Chapter 3: The Sexualization of Touch and Its Impact on Men	39
Chapter 4: Breaking the Chains of Shame	47
Part 2: Stories of Men in Need	**53**
Chapter 5: The Divorced Dad	55
Chapter 6: On, Off, and In Between	61
Chapter 7: The Overlooked Caregiver	67
Chapter 8: Connection Lost, Connection Found	73
Chapter 9: When Love Feels Incomplete	81
Chapter 10: Reaching Across Time	87
Chapter 11: The Strain of Success	93
Chapter 12: Reclaiming the Pieces	99
Chapter 13: Redefining the Mirror	105
Chapter 14: The Courage to Be Both	111
Chapter 15: The Quiet Weight of Loss	117

Part 3: The Unique Challenges Men Face — **123**

Chapter 16: Breaking Through the Shame — 125

Chapter 17: Masculinity and Intimacy — 131

Chapter 18: The Role of Consent and Boundaries for Men — 137

Chapter 19: The Role of Platonic Intimacy in Healthy Relationships — 143

Chapter 20: Dispelling the Shadows — 151

Chapter 21: Why Some Men Seek a Male Touch and Intimacy Coach — 159

Part 4: A New Vision for Male Connection — **165**

Chapter 22: What I've Learned About Men — 167

Chapter 23: Changing the Narrative — 173

Chapter 24: A Vision for a New Masculinity — 181

Chapter 25: Building a Touch-Supportive Community — 189

Chapter 26: A Guide to Healthy Touch — 197

A Call to Connection — 205

Epilogue — 211

Extras — 215

FAQ: Common Questions About Professional Intimacy Services — 219

On Being Seen

To be seen, truly seen,
is to stand naked,
to let the light
fall on the tender places
we so often hide.

— R. Ayité Okyne

*Loneliness is not the absence of people;
it is the absence of connection.
And connection begins
when we dare to reach,
when we dare to be held.*

— R. Ayité Okyne

Prologue

Touch is one of the most fundamental ways we connect with the world—and yet, for so many men, it's a language they've been taught to silence.

Over the years, I've had the privilege of working with men from all walks of life: fathers, executives, young men searching for purpose, and older gentlemen longing for connection. They've come to me carrying stories of strength and struggle, shame and resilience, longing and hope. What they all had in common was a need—sometimes unspoken, sometimes deeply buried—to be seen.

On Being Seen is about more than just physical touch. It's about being acknowledged for who you are, in all your complexity, without judgment. It's about allowing yourself to be vulnerable, to let down the walls that keep you from the connection you crave. And for many men, that first step—asking for touch, admitting a need—is the hardest.

I know firsthand how transformative this journey can be. Touch is not just a physical sensation; it's a bridge between people, a way of saying *I see you, I care about you, you matter*. But for so many men, reaching out for that kind of connection feels like crossing a chasm. The fear of being judged, the weight of societal expectations, and the shame that often surrounds vulnerability can make asking for something as simple as a hug feel impossibly difficult.

That's why I wrote this book.

Through these pages, I want to share the stories of the men I've worked with—not just to shine a light on their courage, but to show that their struggles are not unique. These are stories of men who dared to seek connection in a world that often tells them to go without. They are stories of healing, growth, and transformation.

This book is also an invitation. Whether you're a man searching for connection, someone who loves and cares for the men in your life, or simply curious about the role touch plays in our emotional and physical well-being, I hope you'll find something here that resonates with you.

We live in a world that often values stoicism over softness, independence over intimacy. But I believe there's another way—a way where strength and vulnerability can coexist, where connection is celebrated, and where touch is recognized for the powerful, healing force that it is.

At its core, *On Being Seen* is about reclaiming the parts of yourself that have been hidden for too long. It's about understanding that being vulnerable is not a weakness, but a profound act of courage. And it's about discovering that when you allow yourself to be truly seen, you open the door to deeper relationships, greater self-awareness, and a more fulfilling life.

So, let's begin. Let's explore what it means to be human, to be vulnerable, and to embrace the connections that make life worth living.

Welcome to this journey. Thank you for taking it with me.

On Being Seen

On Being Seen

My Personal Struggle with Touch and Intimacy

Everyone has a story. Before we get into the stories of the men I've worked with, here is my story:

Growing up, touch was a natural part of my childhood. Hugs from my parents, holding hands as we crossed the street, and the occasional cuddle on the couch were all there, woven into the fabric of daily life. But as I grew older, those moments became fewer and farther between. It wasn't something anyone talked about or even noticed—it just happened. My parents, like many, likely assumed I didn't need that kind of affection anymore. Maybe they thought I'd outgrown it. But the truth is, I hadn't.

Then there was intimacy—or, more accurately, the lack of it. I grew up steeped in the British tradition of the "stiff upper lip," where emotions were kept in check and vulnerability was a sign of weakness. There wasn't much room for open-hearted conversations or the kind of connection that comes from sharing your innermost thoughts. Add to that my sexuality as a gay man, and things became even more complicated.

I learned early on that I didn't quite fit the mold of what a man was "supposed" to be. Society had a very clear picture of masculinity—stoic, self-sufficient, and emotionally impenetrable—and I did my best to emulate it. I created a persona that I thought would help me survive in a world that didn't feel particularly welcoming. I was just warm enough to be charming but careful not to let anyone too close. My emotional communication skills were... let's say underdeveloped.

And then there was this strange feedback I kept getting: people told me I came across as "innocent." It wasn't a compliment, exactly, but more of an observation. I think what they meant was that I seemed sexless, untouched by desire or longing. But that couldn't have been further from the truth. Beneath the surface, I was yearning—for connection, for touch, for intimacy—but I didn't know how to ask for it.

My life as a traveler and nomad of sorts added another dimension to this story. I'm a "Third Culture Kid," a term for people who grow up in cultures outside their parents' home country. I've lived in six countries, each with its own cultural attitudes toward touch and intimacy. In some places, touch was casual and abundant—friends walking arm in arm, kisses on the cheek, affectionate pats on the shoulder. In others, touch was reserved, almost clinical. These shifts made it harder to form deep connections, which require time and trust. I became adept at adapting to new environments but struggled to build lasting, meaningful bonds.

When I moved to the U.S. in 2004, I became acutely aware of the prohibitions around touch. My natural touchy-feely disposition suddenly felt out of place, and I found myself pulling back, adjusting to fit in with a culture that often views touch with suspicion or hesitation, or as sexual. This tension between my innate need for connection and the social rules around touch left me feeling a little lost.

In 2018, I stumbled across an article in *The Guardian* about touch therapy. It piqued my curiosity and led me down a rabbit hole of research. I read everything I could find about the science of touch—how it reduces stress, builds trust, and strengthens bonds. I discovered the profound importance of touch in human well-being and how many of us are touch-deprived without even realizing it.

That article changed my life. It gave me a language for something I'd always felt but couldn't articulate. It also planted the seed of an idea—that touch, far from being a secondary need, is central to our emotional and physical health. That realization set me on a path that eventually led to the work I do today.

It's taken me a long time to unlearn the lessons I was socialized with. To shake off the expectations that society placed on me and the ones I placed on myself. I'm well into my adult years now, and I still don't claim to have all the answers. But I'm on a daily mission to be a better man—not by society's standards, but by my own.

Part of that mission has been reclaiming touch and intimacy in my life. I've learned to ask for what I need, even when it feels vulnerable. I've learned to let people in, to share my emotions, and to trust that doing so doesn't make me weak—it makes me human.

This journey hasn't been easy, and it's far from over. But every day, I feel a little more like myself. A little more connected to the man I want to be. And if there's one thing I've learned, it's that we're never done growing.

Touch and intimacy are powerful forces. They've shaped my journey in ways I never expected, and they continue to teach me every day. My hope is that by sharing my story, I can inspire others to reflect on their own relationship with touch and to take steps—however small—toward a life that feels more connected, more authentic, and more alive.

If you're reading this and feeling like parts of my story resonate with your own, I want you to know you're not alone. It's okay to feel like you don't have it all figured out. What matters is that you're trying, that you're showing up for yourself, and that you're open to the possibility of change.

Because at the end of the day, intimacy—whether with others or with ourselves—isn't about perfection. It's about presence. It's about showing up, flaws and all, and saying, *"This is me. I'm here. And I'm ready to connect."*

On Being Seen

On Being Seen

A Hand to Hold

I'll never forget the moment Daniel walked through my door.

He was tall, mid-40s, dressed in a crisp button-down shirt that screamed "business professional," yet his shoulders sagged like he was carrying the weight of the world. His handshake was firm but fleeting, and his eyes darted nervously around the room. I could tell he was trying to play it cool, but underneath the polished exterior was someone who wasn't sure if he belonged here—or anywhere, for that matter.

"I'm not even sure what I'm doing here," he muttered as he sat on the edge of the couch, keeping as much distance between us as possible. "This... isn't something I ever thought I'd do."

I smiled gently. "A lot of people feel that way at first. Take your time. There's no pressure here."

He nodded, his gaze fixed on his hands clasped tightly in his lap. It was a common start. Men like Daniel often come to me with the same mix of apprehension and vulnerability, unsure of how to reconcile their need for connection with the societal voice in their heads telling them they shouldn't have it.

As we began to talk, the story spilled out. Daniel had recently gone through a messy divorce. His ex-wife had been his main source of emotional and physical connection, and now, for the first time in two decades, he was completely alone. His friends meant well, but their solution was always the same: "Hit the gym," "Go on some dates," or "Man up, bro." None of it helped. He was touch-starved, though he didn't have the words for it. He only knew that he felt hollow.

"I don't even know what I need," he admitted after a long pause.

"I think you do," I said softly. "You just haven't given yourself permission to need it."

He looked up at me then, his brow furrowed. It was a look I recognized—a mix of skepticism and the faintest flicker of hope. "What does that even mean?"

"It means we can start slow. You don't have to figure it all out today."

We started with the simplest thing: sitting side by side, fully clothed, with his hand resting on mine. At first, he was stiff, as if he were waiting for some punchline or hidden catch. But as the minutes passed, I could feel his hand begin to relax. His breathing slowed. The tension in his shoulders eased, bit by bit, as he let himself sink into the moment.

"Is this... normal?" he asked quietly.

"It's human," I said.

In that hour, Daniel didn't have to be the man who had it all together. He didn't have to be the strong one, the provider, the fixer. He just got to be Daniel—someone who needed a safe space to feel cared for, held, and accepted without judgment.

By the end of our session, he sat back and exhaled a long, shaky breath. "I didn't realize how much I missed this," he said, almost to himself.

"You're not alone in that," I replied. "A lot of people—especially men—don't realize how much they've been missing until they finally have it again."

Daniel kept coming back, and over time, I watched him transform. He began to carry himself differently—less like a man weighed down by invisible chains and more like someone who had finally started to breathe again.

I share his story not because it's unique but because it's not. There are so many Daniels out there—men who feel isolated, touch-starved, and unsure of where to turn. They've been taught that needing connection makes them weak or broken when, in reality, it makes them human.

This work has taught me that sometimes the simplest act—a hand to hold, a moment of stillness—can make all the difference in the world. And in those quiet moments, when a man like Daniel finally lets himself be vulnerable, I'm reminded why I do this.

Because no one should have to go through life without knowing the power of being cared for, just as they are.

Why This Book Matters

When I first started this work, I knew I was stepping into something unusual—maybe even misunderstood. The idea of professional intimacy services, whether it's cuddle therapy, massage, or sacred intimacy, makes some people uncomfortable. Others simply don't understand it. But as I met client after client, one thing became strikingly clear: we live in a society where men, in particular, are starving for connection, touch, and intimacy, yet they often feel like they aren't allowed to ask for it.

Let's be honest—men are up against a lot when it comes to intimacy. From the time they're boys, they're told to "man up," to "be strong," to suppress their feelings. Vulnerability is often seen as a weakness, and needing something as basic as a hug or a reassuring hand on the shoulder? That can feel, to some men, like admitting failure.

I've heard it so many times in different ways:

"I didn't realize how much I needed this until I felt it."

"I just don't get this kind of touch in my life."

"I'm not sure it's okay for me to want this."

These aren't just passing comments. They're windows into the emotional lives of men who, in many cases, have gone years—sometimes decades—without the kind of connection that makes us feel human.

Think about it. In most cultures, men's opportunities for platonic touch disappear after childhood. While women can hug their friends, hold hands, or offer comfort freely, men are often taught to keep their distance. And if a man does seek out touch, there's an immediate assumption that it must be sexual.

But what happens when a man just wants to be held? When he's not looking for sex, but for comfort?

These are the questions that drove me to write this book.

The Epidemic of Loneliness

We're living in what many experts are calling a loneliness epidemic, and men are at the center of it. Research shows that men are more likely than women to struggle with social isolation, and as they age, their support systems tend to shrink. Friendships drift apart. Romantic relationships end. And all the while, men are less likely to reach out for help.

I've seen this firsthand with my clients. Take, for example, the divorced father who spent years focusing on his kids and career, only to wake up one day and realize he didn't have a single close friend he could turn to. Or the older gentleman who lost his wife and suddenly found himself alone for the first time in 40 years.

Loneliness isn't just about being alone. It's about feeling like no one sees you or understands you. It's about the quiet ache of going through life without the small, everyday connections that remind you that you matter.

The Role of Touch

Touch is one of the most fundamental ways we connect as humans. From the moment we're born, touch tells us we're safe, we're loved, and we belong. But somewhere along the way, many men lose access to that lifeline.

Think about it: when was the last time you hugged a male friend? Not a quick bro-pat-on-the-back kind of hug, but a real, meaningful embrace? When was the last time you rested your head on someone's shoulder, or simply held someone's hand without worrying what it might "mean"?

For many men, the answer is "I can't remember."

It's not just sad—it's harmful. Studies have shown that regular, affectionate touch can lower stress, reduce anxiety, and even improve physical health. But when men don't get that touch, they often turn to substitutes: drinking, working too much, lots of casual meaningless sex, or shutting down emotionally.

This isn't because men are broken. It's because they've been taught that their needs don't matter—or worse, that their needs are shameful.

The Myth of the Strong, Independent Man

One of the biggest hurdles men face is the cultural myth of the "strong, independent man." You know the type—the stoic hero who doesn't cry, doesn't ask for help, and certainly doesn't need anyone.

The problem with this myth is that it's just that: a myth. No one is truly independent. We're wired for connection. And yet, so many men feel trapped by this ideal, afraid to admit that they need the very thing we all need: closeness.

I've worked with men who didn't know how to ask for a hug. Men who felt ashamed to say they were lonely. Men who had no idea where to start when it came to rebuilding their sense of intimacy.

This book is for them—and for anyone who loves them.

A New Way Forward

The purpose of this book isn't just to tell stories, though I hope the stories resonate with you. It's to start a conversation about what men need and why it's okay to need it.

It's okay to want touch without it being sexual.
It's okay to ask for connection without it being a sign of weakness.
It's okay to prioritize your emotional and physical well-being, even if the world around you says you shouldn't.

Through the stories in these pages, I hope to show that seeking intimacy—whether through a hug, a conversation, or a professional service—is one of the most human things you can do.

I hope these stories inspire you to look at the men in your life differently. Maybe even to look at yourself differently. And, most of all, I hope they remind you that no matter how disconnected you feel, you're not alone.

If nothing else, let this book be a hand on your shoulder, a quiet reassurance that it's okay to need what you need. Because every man deserves to feel cared for, seen, and understood. And it's never too late to start.

On Being Seen

Part 1: The Silent Struggles of Men

"What cannot be said will be wept."

— Sappho

Chapter 1: A Culture of Disconnection

Let me start by saying this: the men I work with are some of the bravest people I know. That might surprise you. After all, society rarely equates bravery with vulnerability. But in my experience, it takes real courage to walk into a space like mine, admit you're lonely, or need touch, and ask for connection.

For many men, the simple act of seeking help feels like a betrayal of everything they've been taught about what it means to be "a man."

But what happens when life throws something at you that you can't handle alone? What happens when you're struggling, but you've spent years—or decades—being told that admitting you need anything from anyone makes you weak?

The "Man Box"

There's a concept called the "Man Box," coined by sociologists, that sums this up perfectly. The Man Box is the set of cultural expectations placed on men: be tough, be stoic, be in control. Show no fear, no sadness, no need for comfort. Stay inside the box, and you're a "real man." Step outside of it, and you risk being labeled weak, soft, or even unmanly.

Think about the messages boys receive growing up. Be tough. Don't cry. Don't ask for help. Handle it yourself. These lessons are woven into everything from playground banter to action movies to the way fathers and sons interact. The message is clear: being a man means being strong, stoic, and self-reliant.

One client, Michael, shared a story with me during one of our sessions. As a child, he used to run to his mom for hugs when he felt scared or upset. One day, his dad caught him and pulled him aside. "You're too old for that," his dad said firmly. "Toughen up." Michael was eight.

"I didn't think much of it at the time," Michael told me. "But looking back, that was the moment I stopped asking for hugs."

Michael's story isn't unique. For many men, this conditioning follows them into adulthood. They learn to suppress their emotional needs, and over time, they forget how to ask for connection—or even recognize that they need it.

The Weight of Masculinity

One of the first clients I ever worked with was a man named Rob. Rob was in his early 50s, a retired firefighter, and the very picture of the "strong, silent type." He had a firm handshake, a deep voice, and a way of sitting that made him look like he was ready to spring into action at any moment.

But Rob wasn't here to save anyone. He was here because he couldn't sleep, couldn't focus, and couldn't stop feeling like something was missing.

"I feel ridiculous even being here," he admitted during our first session.

"Why is that?" I asked.

He shrugged, staring at the floor. "Because this isn't what men do. I've always been the guy people rely on. I don't know how to be the one who needs something."

Rob's story isn't unique. In fact, it's one of the most common themes I hear from men. For so long, they've been told their value lies in what they can provide—strength, solutions, protection. There's no room in that narrative for being held, being comforted, or simply being seen.

Touch-Starved and Silent

Rob eventually told me that the last time he could remember being hugged was at his wife's funeral, three years earlier. Before that, he couldn't recall a single moment of non-sexual touch.

"That's just not something guys do," he said.

But why not?

The truth is, many men grow up without examples of what healthy, platonic touch looks like. They're taught to keep their hands to themselves, to avoid anything that could be perceived as "weak" or "too emotional." Over time, they learn to associate touch and intimacy with either romance or weakness, leaving a huge gap in their emotional lives.

And that gap? It's not just emotional. It's physical. Science shows that touch is vital for our well-being. It lowers stress, reduces anxiety, and even helps us live longer. Without it, people often feel disconnected—not just from others, but from themselves.

The Cost of Disconnection

Another client, Jake, was in his late 20s and had just moved to the city for a high-powered job. On paper, he was living the dream: great salary, a downtown apartment, and all the gadgets money could buy. But when Jake sat down in my office, he looked more like someone who hadn't slept in days.

"I don't know why I'm here," he said, running a hand through his hair. "I guess I just feel... off. Like I'm doing everything I'm supposed to, but I still feel empty."

As we talked, it became clear that Jake's "dream life" was also incredibly isolating. He spent his days coding alone, his evenings swiping through dating apps, and his weekends binge-watching Netflix. The only physical contact he had was the occasional handshake or a brush against a stranger.

When I suggested that he might be touch-starved, Jake laughed nervously. "That's a thing?"

It is.

Breaking the Silence

What struck me most about Jake and Rob—and so many of the men I've worked with—is how reluctant they were to name what they were feeling. It wasn't just that they were lonely or touch-starved; it was that they didn't think they were allowed to admit it.

That's the power of the "strong, silent type" archetype. It teaches men to keep their struggles to themselves, to avoid asking for help, and to power through no matter what. But the cost of that silence is enormous.

When men can't express their need for connection, they often channel their pain into other outlets: overworking, drinking, numbing out with TV or video games. Some withdraw entirely, while others lash out in anger or frustration.

The irony is, the very things society discourages—vulnerability, openness, and seeking connection—are the things that could actually help.

The "Strong, Silent Type" in Action

The archetype of the "strong, silent type" is everywhere in our culture. It's the stoic hero in the movies, the unflappable dad who never cries, the boss who never lets his guard down. And while there's nothing inherently wrong with being strong or reserved, the problem comes when these traits are seen as the only acceptable way to be a man.

Take someone like Greg, another client who came to see me after his wife filed for divorce. Greg was in his early 40s, a construction manager, and the kind of guy who prided himself on his no-nonsense attitude.

"I don't know what went wrong," he said during our first session. "I did everything right. I provided for my family, I kept my emotions in check, I never burdened my wife with my problems. But now she's telling me I was distant and unavailable. What does that even mean?"

Greg's story broke my heart because it reflected such a common misunderstanding. He thought he was doing the right thing by being the strong, silent provider, but in reality, his wife felt emotionally abandoned. He wasn't distant because he didn't care—he was distant because he'd been taught that showing vulnerability wasn't an option.

The Ripple Effects of Disconnection

The truth is, this culture of disconnection doesn't just hurt men—it hurts everyone around them. Partners, children, friends, and colleagues all feel the ripple effects of a man who's been taught to suppress his emotional and physical needs.

But the impact on the men themselves is devastating. Loneliness and isolation don't just lead to emotional pain; they can also have serious consequences for physical health. Studies have shown that chronic loneliness can increase the risk of heart disease, depression, and even early death.

And yet, many men don't even realize they're lonely.

One client, Sam, described it like this: "I didn't know I was lonely because I've always been like this. I've always been the guy who goes to work, comes home, and does his own thing. It wasn't until I came here and felt what connection could be like that I realized how much I was missing."

Touch as a Lifeline

Touch is one of the most immediate and powerful ways to bridge the gap of disconnection. It's universal, primal, and something we all crave—even if we don't always admit it.

When I first started working with Rob, the firefighter I mentioned earlier, he was visibly uncomfortable with the idea of touch. During our first session, he sat stiffly on the couch, his arms crossed tightly over his chest.

"This feels... weird," he admitted.

I reassured him that it was okay to feel that way, and we took things slow. Over time, Rob began to relax. He started to open up, and by our fourth session, he allowed himself to lean into a simple embrace.

The change was profound.

"I didn't realize how much I needed this," Rob said quietly. "It's like a part of me that's been asleep is finally waking up."

Reclaiming Connection

The men I work with aren't broken, and they don't need fixing. What they need is permission to reconnect—with themselves, with others, and with the simple, human experiences of touch and intimacy.

This chapter isn't just about pointing out the problem—it's about starting a dialogue. It's about asking why our culture makes it so hard for men to express their need for connection and what we can do to change that.

Because here's the truth: connection isn't a weakness. It's a strength. Allowing yourself to be seen, to ask for what you need, and to receive it—that's where real courage lies.

To the men reading this: If you've ever felt disconnected, lonely, or unsure how to ask for more, you're not alone. It's not just you. It's the culture we've all been shaped by, and it can be unlearned.

To everyone else: Let's challenge the narrative that men should "go it alone." Let's create spaces where vulnerability is met with empathy and where connection is seen as the strength it truly is.

Because in the end, we're all human—and humans aren't meant to live without touch, intimacy, or connection. It's time to break the silence and step out of the Man Box. Together, we can build a culture where everyone, including men, feels seen, valued, and connected.

On Being Seen

Chapter 2: Touch Hunger in Men

Let's talk about something most of us don't think about until it's missing: touch. It's easy to underestimate the power of physical contact because, for many people, it's as much a part of life as breathing or eating. But what happens when touch is absent, when it becomes a rare or even nonexistent part of someone's experience?

For men, in particular, the absence of touch can create a deep, unspoken void—a phenomenon often called "touch hunger." And let me tell you, it's not just emotional. The effects ripple through the body and mind in ways that can't be ignored.

The Science of Touch

Here's what we know about touch: It's fundamental to human well-being. Physical contact releases oxytocin, a hormone sometimes called the "love hormone" or "bonding hormone." Oxytocin helps lower stress, regulate blood pressure, and promote feelings of safety and trust.

Touch also reduces levels of cortisol, the body's primary stress hormone, and increases the release of serotonin and dopamine, which boost mood. In short, touch isn't just nice to have—it's biologically essential.

But when someone is deprived of touch, the opposite can happen. Touch deprivation has been linked to increased stress, anxiety, depression, and even physical health problems like weakened immunity and cardiovascular issues. It's no wonder researchers have likened chronic loneliness to smoking 15 cigarettes a day in terms of its impact on health.

Why Men Are More Prone to Touch Hunger

Touch hunger isn't just a human issue; it's a gendered one. Society has a way of separating men from platonic, nurturing touch early in life. Boys might receive cuddles and hugs as children, but as they grow up, they're often expected to "toughen up" and become independent.

Think about the average teenage boy. How often do you see boys hugging their friends or seeking comfort from a parent? The older they get, the less acceptable it becomes to express affection through touch—unless it's through a firm handshake or a high-five after a sports game.

By the time men reach adulthood, many find themselves in a touch desert. For some, the only acceptable forms of touch are sexual or professional—a pat on the back from a boss, a handshake during a meeting, or intimacy with a partner. But what happens when a man doesn't have a partner or when his relationship lacks physical affection?

This was the case for Brian, a client I'll never forget.

Brian's Story

Brian was in his late 50s when he came to see me. Divorced for nearly a decade, he described himself as a "self-sufficient guy" who didn't need much from anyone. He had a successful career, a few close friends, and a busy schedule. But there was something missing—something he couldn't quite put his finger on.

"It sounds silly," he said during our first session, "but I think I miss being touched."

He told me that after his divorce, he'd stopped dating. His friendships, while meaningful, weren't physically affectionate. "I shake hands with people," he said with a laugh, "but that's about it."

During our first session, Brian was hesitant. He sat at the edge of the couch, his body stiff and his hands clasped tightly in his lap. When I suggested starting with a simple, platonic hug, he hesitated.

"I'm not sure I'm ready for that," he admitted.

We started small. For our first few sessions, Brian and I focused on mindfulness exercises to help him connect with his body. Gradually, he began to open up to the idea of touch.

The breakthrough came during a session when Brian allowed himself to fully lean into a supportive embrace. He held on for what felt like minutes, and when he finally let go, his eyes were brimming with tears.

"I didn't realize how much I needed that," he said softly. "It's like a part of me that's been locked away is finally waking up."

Over time, Brian shared how the absence of touch had affected him. "I thought I was just used to being alone," he said, "but now I see that I was starving for connection—and I didn't even know it."

The Healing Power of Non-Sexual Touch

Brian's experience isn't unique. For many men, non-sexual touch offers a kind of healing they didn't know they needed. It provides a space to feel seen, valued, and cared for without the pressure to perform or meet expectations.

What's remarkable is how quickly the benefits of touch can manifest. Clients often describe feeling lighter, more relaxed, and more grounded after just one session. Some say it's the first time in years they've felt truly at ease in their own skin.

Non-sexual touch creates a bridge between isolation and connection. It reminds men that they're not alone, that their needs are valid, and that it's okay to seek comfort.

Breaking the Stigma Around Male Touch

One of the biggest hurdles to addressing touch hunger in men is the stigma surrounding male vulnerability. Many men worry that seeking out touch will make them seem weak or unmanly. Some fear being judged or misunderstood, especially in a world where physical affection between men is often hypersexualized.

But here's the thing: Touch is a basic human need. It doesn't matter how strong, independent, or self-sufficient you are—your body and mind are wired to crave connection.

I've seen clients from all walks of life—CEOs, construction workers, artists, and athletes—grapple with touch hunger. What they all have in common is the courage to acknowledge their need for connection and take steps to fulfill it.

Chapter 3: The Sexualization of Touch and Its Impact on Men

Let's be honest—our culture has a touch problem. It's not that touch is missing entirely, but that it's been narrowly defined and, more often than not, sexualized. For men especially, this creates a world where physical affection is limited, misunderstood, and sometimes outright feared.

As someone who works intimately with men seeking connection and healing, I see firsthand how the sexualization of touch impacts their lives. It creates confusion, shame, and barriers to the kind of human connection we all need to thrive. Let's unpack how this came to be and what it means for men today.

How Touch Became Sexualized

It's no secret that touch, one of the most natural and universal human experiences, has become deeply entwined with sexuality in modern culture. Somewhere along the way, we lost sight of touch as a form of connection, comfort, and care, and began to view it almost exclusively through a sexual lens. This shift didn't happen overnight—it's the result of cultural, historical, and societal forces that have shaped the way we relate to our bodies and to one another.

In many Western cultures, the Victorian era marked a turning point. Public displays of affection, even among family members, were frowned upon, and physical touch became associated with impropriety. Over time, this prudishness gave way to a more open discussion of sexuality, but the pendulum swung so far in the other direction that touch became almost synonymous with sexual expression.

The rise of mass media in the 20th century further reinforced this association. Movies, television, and advertising often portrayed touch in highly sexualized contexts, leaving little room for platonic or nurturing forms of physical contact. The result? A cultural narrative that suggests if someone touches you—or if you touch someone else—it must have sexual undertones.

Layered on top of this is the fear of inappropriate touch, which has grown in recent decades due to increased awareness of abuse and harassment. While this awareness is crucial and necessary, it has also led to a heightened sense of caution, making people hesitant to engage in touch that could be misinterpreted.

In the United States, this caution is particularly pronounced. Having lived in six different countries, I've seen firsthand how attitudes toward touch vary. In some cultures, touch is woven into daily interactions—friends holding hands, colleagues embracing, family members freely expressing affection. But in the U.S., touch is often reserved for romantic or sexual relationships, with little space for platonic physical connection.

The impact of this sexualization of touch is profound. Many people are touch-deprived without even realizing it. They crave connection but don't know how to ask for it, fearing that their intentions will be misunderstood. This deprivation can lead to feelings of isolation, loneliness, and even physical and emotional health issues.

For men, this conflation is compounded by rigid gender norms. Many are taught from a young age that their worth is tied to strength, independence, and stoicism. Showing affection or seeking non-sexual touch doesn't align with these ideals. As a result, physical contact becomes limited to two main contexts:

Romantic and Sexual Relationships: Men are expected to reserve physical touch for partners, reinforcing the idea that all touch is inherently sexual.

Sports or Professional Interactions: Even here, touch is carefully controlled—think of a quick handshake, a backslap, or a team huddle. It's brief, functional, and often void of emotional depth.

This leaves little room for platonic, nurturing touch, which is essential for emotional well-being.

The good news is that we can reclaim touch. We can learn to see it as more than a precursor to sex—as a language of care, compassion, and connection. Touch can be a hug from a friend, a comforting hand on the shoulder, or the simple act of sitting close to someone you trust. It doesn't have to mean anything more than, "I'm here. You're not alone."

By redefining our relationship with touch, we can begin to break free from the narrow, sexualized framework that limits us. We can create a culture where touch is safe, consensual, and deeply human—a culture where touch can heal, nurture, and bring us closer together.

The Negative Effects of Sexualizing Touch

When touch is primarily viewed through a sexual lens, it creates several challenges for men:

Fear of Being Misunderstood: Many men hesitate to express physical affection toward friends, family, or even their children because they worry it will be misinterpreted. A father might avoid hugging his teenage son too often, fearing it will seem inappropriate. A man might refrain from comforting a male friend with a touch on the shoulder, worrying it will be seen as gay, romantic, or unmanly.

Shame Around Physical Needs: The sexualization of touch can make men feel ashamed of their natural desire for connection. Wanting a hug or a comforting touch might seem weak, needy, or even perverse in a society that equates masculinity with emotional self-sufficiency.

Emotional Isolation: Without access to platonic touch, many men experience a profound sense of loneliness. They might not even realize that part of what they're missing is physical connection because the idea of non-sexual touch isn't normalized.

Strained Relationships: Men who rely solely on romantic partners for physical affection can unintentionally place a heavy burden on those relationships. When touch needs are unmet elsewhere, it creates pressure for partners to fulfill all aspects of emotional and physical connection, which isn't sustainable.

A Client's Story: Jason's Journey

Jason came to see me after a friend recommended my services. In his early 40s, Jason was outgoing, funny, and seemingly confident. But as he sat across from me in our first session, his words revealed a different story.

"I've been single for three years," he said, his voice hesitant. "And, honestly, I think I've forgotten what it feels like to be touched."

He explained that after his last relationship ended, he'd thrown himself into work and hobbies, keeping busy to avoid confronting his loneliness. But no matter how full his schedule became, something always felt missing.

"I didn't realize how much I relied on my ex for... everything," he admitted. "It wasn't just about sex. It was about the little things—holding hands, cuddling on the couch, even a quick hug before work. Without that, I feel... hollow."

Jason hesitated before adding, "I'm almost embarrassed to be here. What kind of man pays for a hug?"

His words broke my heart because they echoed what so many clients have told me: that their need for touch feels shameful or taboo.

During our sessions, Jason began to untangle the confusion he felt about touch. He started to see that his need for connection wasn't a weakness or a failure—it was a fundamental part of being human.

One day, after a particularly emotional session, Jason said something that stayed with me. "You know, I always thought touch was about sex. But now I see it's so much more than that. It's about feeling like I matter."

Reframing Touch as a Human Need

Jason's experience highlights a crucial point: touch isn't inherently sexual. It can be comforting, grounding, and healing without any romantic or sexual connotations.

By reframing touch as a basic human need rather than a sexual act, we can help men break free from the shame and confusion they often feel.

Here are some ways we can shift the narrative:

Normalize Platonic Touch: Encourage men to hug their friends, hold their children, or offer a comforting pat on the back without fear of judgment.

Educate About the Benefits of Touch: Help men understand that touch reduces stress, strengthens relationships, and improves mental health. It's not about weakness—it's about well-being.

Create Safe Spaces for Connection: Services like professional cuddling or mindful intimacy sessions provide a judgment-free environment where men can experience the healing power of touch.

Toward a Healthier View of Touch

The sexualization of touch doesn't just hurt men—it hurts all of us. It isolates people, perpetuates stereotypes, and prevents meaningful connection.

But we have the power to change this. By challenging the idea that touch is always sexual, we can create a culture where men feel free to seek and give affection without fear or shame.

To the men reading this: You deserve connection. You deserve to feel seen, valued, and cared for. And it's okay to want that—it's okay to need it.

Touch isn't about being strong or weak. It's about being human.

Chapter 4: Breaking the Chains of Shame

Let's talk about something that isn't always easy to discuss, but is so important: the role homophobia—both external and internalized—plays in shaping how men experience touch and connection.

As a society, we've got a lot of work to do when it comes to how we treat men, especially when it comes to the intersections of masculinity, sexuality, and touch. For many men, whether they're straight, gay, bisexual, or questioning, homophobia is a pervasive force that distorts their ability to seek and receive the kind of non-sexual touch we all need. It's a subtle but powerful undercurrent that can be felt in the way men avoid physical affection with one another or how they repress their own desire for it.

It's important to address this because I've seen firsthand how deeply these issues affect men—whether they recognize it or not—and how they shape the way men interact with each other and with themselves.

The Role of Homophobia in Shaping Touch

Homophobia isn't just something that affects gay men; it affects everyone. It creates an environment where touch is weaponized, where anything that might be interpreted as "too affectionate" or "too emotional" is seen as suspect. Men are conditioned to avoid vulnerability, to guard against anything that might make them appear "soft" or, heaven forbid, "gay." The irony, of course, is that the need for affection, for connection, for touch, is universal. But because touch is so often sexualized or associated with queerness, men are trained to suppress it.

For straight men, homophobia can make simple gestures like hugging a friend or placing a hand on someone's shoulder feel dangerous. "What if someone thinks I'm gay?" is a real concern for many men, even in the most platonic of situations. We live in a world that sends the message that touch, unless it's in the context of a sexual or romantic relationship, is a threat to one's masculinity.

This kind of thinking leaves men in a difficult bind. They might crave connection—longing for a simple touch to help them feel grounded and seen—but they are also terrified of being misjudged or misunderstood.

Internalized Homophobia: A Silent Barrier

Now, let's talk about internalized homophobia. This is the internalized belief system that some men, particularly straight-identified men, develop when they've absorbed societal views that equate being gay with something "lesser" or "wrong." Internalized homophobia doesn't just manifest as dislike toward gay people; it can show up in a man's own relationship with his body, his emotions, and his desires for connection.

Internalized homophobia often manifests as a deep reluctance to allow oneself to need physical affection that isn't tied to sex or romance. It becomes easier to keep people at arm's length—literally and emotionally—than to risk being vulnerable or, worse yet, being perceived as "gay." A lot of men end up suppressing their own touch needs, not because they don't want affection, but because they've learned that such needs are shameful or dangerous.

This isn't just theoretical—it plays out in real lives. I've seen it in my practice. Men who have spent their whole lives suppressing their touch hunger, convincing themselves that they don't need it, when deep down, they are starving for connection. These are the men who tell me, "I've never had a friend hug me like that" or "I've always felt uncomfortable hugging other men." The emotional pain caused by this can be overwhelming, and it's a huge part of why so many men struggle with intimacy and loneliness.

A Client's Story: Ben's Awakening

I'll never forget Ben's story. He came to see me after years of struggling with deep loneliness and isolation. In his early 30s, Ben had been raised in a strict household where vulnerability was seen as weakness, and affection—particularly between men—was seen as unnecessary. He had learned that men don't touch other men in a way that could be misinterpreted, even if it was just a hug or a supportive pat on the back.

"I always thought I was fine," he told me. "I mean, I've got friends, I'm social. I've just never been the type to hug or get too close to anyone. It felt... unnatural."

Ben had been told from a young age that real men don't show emotion or need affection. It was so ingrained in him that he couldn't even begin to imagine that something as simple as a hug could be healing. But his isolation had started to take its toll. He was dating someone, but it was clear that the emotional distance in his life was affecting his relationship.

"I've always thought I'd be fine on my own," Ben continued, his voice quieter now, almost sheepish. "But I think I've been so cut off from everything—my emotions, my body—that I don't even know how to connect anymore."

In our sessions, Ben began to confront the wall of internalized homophobia that had prevented him from seeking the kind of touch he needed. He had never allowed himself to experience touch without an agenda or a fear of being seen as "soft." But slowly, as we worked together, he started to realize that seeking and receiving platonic touch didn't threaten his masculinity or his identity as a straight man. In fact, it made him feel more alive, more human.

During one session, Ben hesitated before saying, "I never realized how much I needed just to be held. Just to be cared for without any expectation." That was a breakthrough moment for him. Through the experience of physical connection that wasn't sexual or romantic, he learned that he could receive affection without fear of judgment or shame. He didn't have to hide that part of himself any longer.

Breaking the Cycle: Reclaiming Touch and Connection

It's time to break the cycle. Homophobia—whether external or internalized—doesn't just hurt gay men; it hurts all men. It teaches them to fear the most basic human connection: touch. It sends the message that love, affection, and tenderness are only acceptable in certain contexts—contexts that often exclude men's emotional and physical needs.

By challenging these beliefs, we can create a healthier world where all men feel safe seeking connection, free from the burden of shame and judgment. Men deserve to feel loved, to feel cared for, and to feel that they matter—not because they fit into a rigid mold, but because they are human.

For men like Ben, and for so many others, seeking professional help for touch and connection can be a transformative experience. It allows them to reconnect with their own need for affection, to shed the fear that has held them back, and to finally embrace the truth: touch is a basic need. It's not about sexuality—it's about humanity.

To the men who have internalized these messages of fear and shame, I want you to hear this: It's okay to need touch. It's okay to be vulnerable. You don't need to hide from your need for affection, and you don't need to let anyone else make you feel like you're less of a man because you desire connection. The world is waiting for you to show up, to touch, and to be touched. It's time to reclaim that part of yourself.

Part 2: Stories of Men in Need

"The privilege of a lifetime is to become who you truly are."

— Carl Jung

Chapter 5: The Divorced Dad

Divorce can leave a person feeling fractured, like the foundation of their entire life has been pulled out from under them. It's an emotional earthquake, shaking every part of your identity—your relationship with yourself, with others, and with the world around you. For men, especially, there is often a particular kind of loneliness that comes with divorce. The loss is not just of a partner, but of intimacy, trust, and affection—the very things that help us feel seen and understood.

One of my clients, John, came to me in the aftermath of his divorce. He was a man in his late 40s, a father of two teenage children, and at a crossroads in his life. His marriage had fallen apart a few years ago, but the effects still haunted him. John felt emotionally distant from his ex-wife, but more painfully, he felt disconnected from himself.

"I don't even know who I am anymore," John admitted during our first session. He looked worn out, tired, like the weight of a thousand questions was pressing on him all at once. "I don't trust anyone. I don't trust myself."

John's words weren't unique, but they were deeply familiar. Many men who go through a divorce feel the same way. When you've built your life around someone else and then lose them, it can feel as though you've lost the map to your own heart. The emotional and physical intimacy that was once part of his daily life was suddenly gone, and he had no idea how to rebuild it.

The Struggles After Divorce

For John, the hardest part wasn't the end of his marriage itself, but the aftermath. His trust had been broken—not just in his ex-wife, but in relationships in general. He was no longer sure how to connect with others, whether it was romantic partners or even friends. When you've been hurt, it's easy to slip into the belief that closeness and affection are dangerous, and that the emotional and physical intimacy you once craved is now out of reach.

"Sometimes, I wonder if I'll ever feel that close to someone again," John said. "It's hard to imagine anyone getting that close without me getting hurt, or worse, hurting them."

His fear wasn't just about trust—it was about touch. For years, John had been in a relationship where affection was a routine part of life. But after the divorce, there was no one to hold him, no one to lean on. The simple act of being touched, whether it was a hug, a gentle hand on his back, or even a friendly handshake, became a reminder of what he had lost. And even more, it made him realize how much he was longing for that connection again.

But how could he get it back? How could he open himself up to trust and touch again when it felt so risky?

The Journey to Rebuilding Trust and Affection

Our work together began with the basics. I didn't focus on relationships at first; I focused on John himself. His first assignment was simple: to touch himself. Not in a sexual way, but in a tender, self-compassionate way. I encouraged him to place his hand on his chest or his arm, to close his eyes, and to feel his own body. To reconnect with the sensation of being present in his own skin. This was the first step in helping him understand that touch doesn't always need to come from someone else to be healing—it starts with you.

It was difficult for John at first. He had become so used to pushing his emotions down and avoiding physical touch that even small acts of self-care felt awkward. But over time, John started to soften. He began to allow himself to feel the physical presence of his own body, to treat it with kindness, to acknowledge its needs.

As we continued working together, John opened up about the deeper layers of his struggles. The fear of being hurt again was one thing, but there was also a deep, aching loneliness that he had been hiding. The emotional distance he felt from his ex-wife had created a void inside of him that he didn't know how to fill. He wasn't sure how to meet his own needs for affection anymore, let alone trust someone else to meet them.

Rediscovering Connection

Through our sessions, we gradually worked on building trust, not just with others, but with himself. For John, rediscovering the power of non-sexual touch was a huge breakthrough. The more he allowed himself to experience tenderness without the fear of it turning into something more complicated or intimate, the more he began to soften his barriers. He started to realize that touch wasn't just about sex or romance—it was about human connection, the kind of connection we all need to feel grounded and whole.

One day, he shared an experience with me that seemed small but was profound for him. He had been at a family gathering and had felt an urge to give his teenage son a hug. For years, he had been afraid of expressing that kind of affection because it felt "awkward" or "too much." But something shifted in him that day, and he reached out to hug his son. And his son hugged him back.

"It was like I was touching him and touching myself at the same time," John said, his voice cracking slightly. "I didn't even realize how much I needed it until it happened. I felt like I was reconnecting with something I lost."

It was a simple moment, but it meant everything to John. It was the first time in a long time that he allowed himself to be open to affection without the fear of vulnerability. It wasn't just about giving his son a hug—it was about reconnecting to the part of himself that had been shut off for so long. The part that had once believed that touch could heal.

Rebuilding Trust, Rebuilding Yourself

John's journey didn't stop there. He began to find ways to incorporate more touch into his life—whether it was through giving his friends a hug or allowing himself to feel the comfort of a hand on his back. As he began to rebuild his emotional and physical connections, he also started to trust again. Not just in other people, but in himself.

His relationship with his ex-wife didn't magically heal overnight, but John began to approach it from a place of strength. He realized that he didn't need to close himself off in order to protect himself from pain. Instead, he could allow himself to be vulnerable, knowing that vulnerability is a strength, not a weakness.

And the most beautiful part of this journey was that John started to see that he didn't need to be in a romantic relationship to experience intimacy. He didn't need to wait for someone else to fill the void. The connection he sought was always there, within himself and in the people who truly cared about him.

A New Beginning

John's story is one that I see reflected in many of the men I work with. Divorce, heartbreak, and loss can feel like an end, but they can also be the beginning of something new. When we allow ourselves to reconnect with the simple, powerful act of touch—when we allow ourselves to feel again—we open the door to healing and transformation.

For men like John, rediscovering affection, rebuilding trust, and healing from the wounds of the past isn't just about finding someone to share your life with. It's about reconnecting with yourself and understanding that you are worthy of love, affection, and touch—not because of who you are in a relationship, but because you are human.

If you're reading this and feeling a sense of recognition, know that healing is possible. It's okay to feel vulnerable. It's okay to need connection. And it's okay to seek touch that helps you feel whole again. It's not a weakness; it's part of what makes you beautifully human.

Chapter 6: On, Off, and In Between

When Ethan first walked into my office, he seemed like someone who had everything figured out. He spoke warmly about his husband, James, describing their relationship as a loving, supportive partnership. They had been married for seven years, and Ethan said James was his best friend and his anchor in life.

But as Ethan shared more, he revealed a tension he hadn't yet been able to resolve. "James and I have an amazing relationship," he said, "but there's this one thing I can't seem to get past. I love being touched—it's how I feel most connected—but I struggle to ask for it. And James is just... different."

Ethan described James as an "on/off switch"—someone who was either fully engaged or fully disengaged, especially when it came to physical affection. James was extroverted and gregarious, often moving through the world with the energy of a whirlwind. Ethan, on the other hand, called himself a "dimmer switch." He liked to ease into connection slowly, building up moments of closeness with touch and quiet gestures.

"I get that we're wired differently," Ethan explained, "but sometimes I wish he'd just know when I need him to reach out—to hold me, put his arm around me, anything."

The Reluctance to Ask

When I asked Ethan why he didn't feel comfortable asking for the touch he wanted, he hesitated. "It makes me feel... exposed," he said. "Like I'm admitting I'm needy. And what if he thinks I'm being too much?"

This is something I hear often from men. Despite our progress as a society, many of us still equate asking for emotional or physical support with weakness. Ethan's reluctance wasn't about a lack of love or communication in his marriage—it was about the vulnerability that comes with openly expressing his needs.

Reframing Vulnerability

One of the first things I shared with Ethan was my belief that vulnerability is not a weakness; it's a profound act of courage. By being vulnerable, we allow our relationships to grow deeper and more authentic. Ethan seemed to resonate with this, but I could tell it would take some time for him to truly embrace it.

To start, I introduced him to an exercise I call The Touch Request Practice. It's a simple, structured way to practice asking for touch in a way that feels safe and non-threatening.

The Touch Request Practice

Ethan and I practiced together during our sessions. At first, the requests were small and specific:

"Could you place your hand on my shoulder for a moment?"

"Would you hold my hand while I talk about something difficult?"

"Can we sit next to each other on the couch tonight?"

Ethan admitted he felt awkward at first. "It's like I'm rehearsing how to be needy," he joked.

But as we practiced, Ethan began to see that his requests weren't demands; they were invitations. He wasn't asking James to fix anything or to be someone he wasn't—he was simply sharing a part of himself and allowing James to respond.

Bringing It Home

Ethan took the practice home and started small. One evening, as they were winding down after dinner, Ethan turned to James and said, "Can we sit together on the couch tonight? I'd love it if you held my hand."

He told me later how nervous he'd felt in that moment, but James had simply smiled and said, "Of course."

"That wasn't so bad," Ethan admitted, laughing. "Actually, it felt kind of nice to just say it."

Understanding Each Other's Wiring

Over time, Ethan began to see his and James's differences not as obstacles but as opportunities for connection. He started explaining to James how much he valued touch as a way of feeling connected. James, in turn, began to share how his extroverted energy sometimes left him too drained to think about small gestures of affection.

"It's not that I don't want to," James had said to him one evening. "Sometimes I just don't realize you need it."

That conversation was a turning point for them. Ethan realized that James wasn't withholding touch; he just had a different way of navigating their relationship. And by speaking up, Ethan was giving James the tools to meet him halfway.

Dimmer Switch Meets On/Off Switch

The more Ethan practiced asking for touch, the more natural it felt. And something unexpected started to happen: James began initiating touch more often, without Ethan needing to ask.

"It's like he's learned how to dim his switch a little," Ethan said with a smile.

By normalizing his own needs, Ethan had given James permission to slow down and tune in. They found a rhythm that worked for both of them—one where Ethan could ease into connection and James could find joy in those quiet moments of touch.

Lessons from Ethan

Ethan's story is a reminder that even in the strongest relationships, unspoken needs can create distance. But with a little vulnerability and a lot of communication, those needs can become opportunities for growth.

If you've ever felt hesitant to ask for what you need—whether it's touch, time, or attention—consider this: your needs are not burdens. They are invitations for connection, and expressing them is one of the greatest gifts you can give to someone who loves you.

As Ethan said to me during one of our final sessions: "I thought asking for touch would make me feel smaller. But it's made our relationship bigger."

Chapter 7: The Overlooked Caregiver

I first met Robert on a quiet afternoon in my office. He came in with a calm, almost stoic presence, and it wasn't until we started talking that I realized just how much was going on behind the surface. Robert was in his mid-50s, a widowed father of two young children, and had been carrying the weight of the world on his shoulders for years. He was the sole provider, the protector, the fixer—everything that he believed he had to be in order to give his kids the stability they needed after their mother's sudden death.

What struck me about Robert was his ability to care so deeply for others, while quietly ignoring his own needs. As we spoke, I learned that his days were filled with constant duties: working long hours, attending parent-teacher meetings, running errands, and being there for his kids whenever they needed him. His entire world revolved around making sure everyone else was okay. And yet, there was a quiet desperation in his eyes when he spoke about how much he missed just being cared for.

"I don't even remember the last time someone asked how I was doing," Robert said softly, his voice tinged with frustration. "I'm always the one who takes care of everyone else. But who takes care of me?"

The Burden of the Caregiver

It's a position many men find themselves in: the constant caregiver, the one who puts others first while neglecting their own needs. For Robert, this role had become so ingrained that he didn't even realize how deeply he was suffering from the lack of nurturing touch, affection, and emotional support. He was so focused on ensuring his children felt loved and supported that he had forgotten what it felt like to be on the receiving end of that care.

It's a familiar story for many men who take on the role of the caregiver—whether as a father, a partner, or a friend. Men are often socialized to be the strong one, the provider, the one who holds everything together. Society tells them that their worth is tied to what they give, to their ability to protect and nurture others. But the truth is that this constant self-sacrifice, without any care in return, leaves a person feeling hollow.

When Robert shared his story with me, I could hear the weight in his voice, a deep sense of exhaustion that went beyond physical tiredness. This was emotional depletion—a silent suffering that had been building up for years. As much as he loved his children and was committed to their well-being, he had lost the ability to care for himself.

"I'm running on empty," he admitted. "And I don't know how to fill myself back up."

The Need for Nurturing Touch

I could see in Robert's body language that he longed for touch, but didn't have the vocabulary to ask for it. Men, especially those who take on the role of caregiver, can sometimes feel that any form of receiving care is a sign of weakness. For Robert, the idea of being the one to receive care rather than give it felt like a betrayal of his identity. He was so accustomed to being the strong, self-reliant man that it was difficult for him to imagine himself in a more vulnerable position.

This is where professional intimacy—specifically, the kind of nurturing touch I offer—can be such a powerful tool. Unlike a friend or family member, there is no history, no pressure, and no obligation for him to reciprocate. In our sessions, Robert didn't have to worry about being the "strong one." There was no emotional labor expected of him. Instead, he was allowed to be fully present in the moment and experience the nurturing he had been deprived of for so long.

I gently encouraged Robert to allow himself to relax into the touch and not focus on what he thought he should be feeling. For many men like Robert, the first experience of receiving professional touch can be disorienting. There's a vulnerability that comes with it—an exposure of the heart and body that feels unfamiliar, even risky. But I reminded Robert that this space was created for him to be cared for without judgment, without expectations.

The Healing Power of Being Nurtured

The first time Robert came for a session, he was tentative. His body was stiff, his movements rigid, as though he was unsure how to allow himself to relax. He had spent so many years living in "caregiver mode" that his body had become conditioned to stay tense, to hold everything together. I focused on creating a safe, gentle environment, guiding him to feel at ease with the touch without any strings attached.

After a few moments, Robert finally exhaled deeply. I could feel his body slowly begin to release the tension it had been holding onto for so long. His shoulders dropped, his hands softened. It was as though he was allowing himself to trust in the nurturing energy, to surrender the control he had held onto for years. For the first time in what felt like forever, Robert was no longer the one doing the caring. He was the one being cared for.

"I didn't know I needed this," he said, his voice softer now. "It's like I'm remembering what it feels like to be human again, not just a machine going through the motions."

That was a pivotal moment in our work together. For Robert, it wasn't just the touch that was healing—it was the permission he gave himself to receive. To allow himself the space to be nurtured, without guilt or shame. He began to realize that in order to continue caring for his children and others, he had to first care for himself.

The Power of Self-Care for Caregivers

Over time, Robert started to understand that self-care wasn't selfish. It wasn't a luxury; it was a necessity. As he learned to allow himself to receive nurturing touch and emotional care, he found that he had more energy and patience to give to his children. He wasn't running on empty anymore. Instead, he was filling himself up with the very things he had neglected for so long: affection, kindness, and the permission to be vulnerable.

"I didn't realize how much I was missing until I felt it," Robert said one day, after a few sessions. "I feel like I can be a better father now, because I'm finally giving myself the care I need. And I'm not so afraid to ask for help anymore."

Robert's journey is a reminder that even the strongest caregivers need care. Even those who give so much to others deserve the chance to receive. Professional intimacy, in the form of nurturing touch and emotional support, can offer a rare and invaluable moment for those who are too used to giving everything to others. It's a chance to remember that you are human, and you are worthy of care, just as much as anyone else.

So, to all the caregivers out there—whether you're a father, a partner, a friend, or someone who simply carries the weight of others' well-being on your shoulders—know this: You are allowed to be nurtured. You are allowed to receive. And when you give yourself the care you need, you are not only healing yourself—you're making it possible for you to show up for others in ways you never thought possible.

It's not selfish to care for yourself. It's necessary. And it's the first step toward truly being there for the people who need you most.

Chapter 8: Connection Lost, Connection Found

When I first met Sam, he was in his late 20s, a millennial trying to navigate life in a world that seemed to move faster than he could keep up with. Sam had all the outward signs of success: a decent job, a decent social media following, and a busy calendar filled with activities. But beneath all that, there was a sense of loneliness he couldn't shake. It wasn't the kind of loneliness that comes from being alone in a room; it was the quiet, constant ache of being surrounded by people but feeling invisible.

In the midst of a world that is more connected than ever through technology, Sam felt more disconnected than he ever had before.

"I have all these friends online," Sam said as we sat down for our first session, his voice carrying a mix of frustration and confusion. "But when I actually sit down and think about it, I feel like I don't really know anyone. It's like everything's a performance. I keep swiping, liking, messaging, but none of it feels real."

As we talked, I realized that Sam was like many young men today, caught in the whirlwind of social media and hookup culture. These platforms promise connection but often deliver isolation. The "likes," the DMs, the brief encounters—while they might feel like a form of validation or intimacy, they never quite satisfy the deeper need for genuine connection.

The Pressure of Social Media

Social media is often seen as the place to be seen, to feel validated, to connect. It's easy to fall into the trap of believing that the number of followers or likes you get translates into real relationships. Sam was no different. His Instagram feed was filled with carefully curated images of nights out, group photos with friends, and moments that screamed "I'm living my best life." On the surface, everything seemed fine. But in reality, the very thing that made him feel popular—being constantly connected—was the same thing that made him feel profoundly lonely.

I asked Sam how many of the people on his social media were people he felt he could truly rely on, people who really knew him. His answer was a slow shake of his head. "Not many. I mean, sure, I have a lot of friends online, but when it comes down to it, I don't know who I could actually talk to when I'm struggling. It's like everything's just... shallow."

The truth is, social media has a way of distorting our sense of intimacy. It fosters the illusion of connection but often leads to a sense of disconnection. People curate their lives, posting only the moments they want others to see, leading to a culture of comparison and inauthenticity. Sam, like many young men, was caught in this cycle. He'd scroll through his feed and see everyone else's seemingly perfect lives, wondering why his didn't measure up.

The problem with this kind of "connection" is that it lacks depth. It's easy to get caught up in the idea that a quick message or a swipe right is enough to fulfill our need for closeness, but these interactions never fill the emotional void. True connection requires vulnerability, trust, and the willingness to show up for someone—not just online, but in person, in real life.

The Toll of Hookup Culture

Beyond the screen, Sam's personal life mirrored the emptiness he felt online. He was active in the world of dating apps, swiping left and right, engaging in casual hookups, but nothing ever lasted beyond a few quick encounters. Each time, he hoped for something more, something that would bring him the intimacy he longed for, but he always ended up feeling more disconnected than before.

"I'm so tired of just having sex and then walking away," Sam confessed. "It's like... we're both pretending that it's fine, but I'm not fine. I don't even know how to talk to someone about what I really want anymore."

Hookup culture, while it can be fun or exciting in the moment, often leaves people feeling more isolated. The expectation of instant gratification—whether it's through a swipe, a message, or a quick hookup—reinforces the idea that intimacy is about physical pleasure, not emotional connection. But for men like Sam, the true longing is for more than just physical touch—it's the need for emotional intimacy, for someone who sees them for who they really are, and someone they can trust.

It's easy to get lost in the cycle of fleeting interactions, especially in a world that has increasingly normalized them. But this way of connecting often leaves men feeling emotionally starved, as if they've been offered a taste of connection but never the full meal.

The Turning Point: Learning to Value Authentic Connection

Sam's turning point came when he realized that the connections he was seeking on his phone were never going to bring him the fulfillment he was longing for. He came to me because he was exhausted from the constant cycle of short-lived interactions and wanted something deeper, something more meaningful. He wanted to experience real intimacy—not the kind that comes with expectations or obligations, but the kind that is grounded in vulnerability, trust, and shared humanity.

We started by exploring what true connection looked like for him. I asked him to think about times when he felt truly seen and heard—not just by a romantic partner, but by a friend, a family member, or even himself. Sam's answers weren't about the grand gestures or the big moments. They were simple: a conversation where someone listened, a hug that didn't come with a hidden agenda, an evening spent talking without worrying about the clock or the next "like."

"I've realized I've been chasing the wrong things," Sam said, his voice quieter this time. "I thought I needed to keep up with everyone else, posting, dating, trying to get the next hit of validation. But all I really want is to feel like I matter to someone. Like I'm more than just an image on a screen."

It was a powerful realization, and it was the beginning of Sam's journey toward valuing authentic connection over superficial interactions. We began working on building real intimacy—emotional, physical, and spiritual. Not through social media, not through dating apps, but through face-to-face interactions where he could truly be himself, where he could allow himself to be vulnerable and open.

A New Way of Being

Over the next few months, Sam began to shift how he approached relationships. He started saying no to hookups that didn't align with his values. Instead, he focused on developing deeper, more authentic connections with the people who truly mattered in his life. He took time to nurture friendships, to have real conversations, and to practice showing up for himself in a way that didn't rely on external validation.

One of the most profound shifts for Sam came when he started allowing himself to be vulnerable in a way he hadn't before. He learned to lean into his need for human connection, and he stopped treating intimacy like a commodity to be consumed. Instead, he began to see it as something sacred—something that required effort, presence, and a willingness to be truly seen.

"That's what I was missing," Sam said, looking back on the journey. "I was so caught up in trying to impress people or show them a version of myself that wasn't real. Now, I'm learning to connect with people on a deeper level, and it feels so much more fulfilling."

The Takeaway: Moving Beyond the Noise

Sam's journey is not unique. So many young men today are caught in the pressure of social media, hookup culture, and the constant need for external validation. But the truth is, real connection cannot be found through a screen or in a fleeting encounter. It requires time, trust, and vulnerability.

If there's one thing I want you to take away from this chapter, it's this: True intimacy is not about instant gratification or the next quick fix. It's about learning to value the moments of real connection—the ones where you can be fully yourself, without the need to impress or perform. It's about cultivating the kind of relationships that nourish you, that help you grow, and that remind you that you're not alone.

So, if you're feeling lost in the noise of modern life, remember this: You don't have to settle for shallow interactions. You deserve more. You deserve real, meaningful connection. And that starts by being brave enough to seek it, even if it feels scary or unfamiliar.

You don't need to chase validation anymore. All you need is the courage to be real.

Chapter 9: When Love Feels Incomplete

I remember sitting with Mark in our session, a man in his early 30s, who came to me with a vulnerability I could feel in the air. He had been with his boyfriend for three years, a relationship that, by all accounts, seemed healthy and loving. They had great conversations, shared common interests, and had built a solid foundation of trust. But despite all that, Mark had been feeling something essential was missing. And it wasn't about sex—it was about touch.

As Mark shared his story, it became clear that he was craving something deeper than what his boyfriend could give him. His words, carefully chosen and tinged with sadness, painted a picture of a relationship where emotional and physical intimacy existed—but only to a certain point.

"I love him," Mark said softly, his voice betraying a sense of longing, "but sometimes I just feel... alone. I don't think he realizes how much I need touch. I don't think he gets how much I need to be held, to be touched, to feel that kind of closeness."

It wasn't that Mark's boyfriend didn't care about him. Quite the opposite. They were deeply committed to one another, but Mark's boyfriend wasn't naturally affectionate in the way that Mark needed. He showed love in his own way —through words, acts of service, and shared moments—but physical touch was something that didn't come as easily to him.

It's easy to think that when you're in a loving, committed relationship, touch and affection should come automatically. But what happens when one person craves that closeness while the other either doesn't know how to give it or feels uncomfortable providing it? What do you do when your love language is touch, but your partner's is something different?

The Unspoken Need for Touch

For Mark, the issue wasn't a lack of love. It wasn't even about his boyfriend's actions, or lack thereof. It was about how their relationship left him feeling emotionally starved, and not just in a casual, passing way. Touch for Mark was a vital part of how he felt loved, how he felt seen and valued. Without it, he felt disconnected, not just from his boyfriend, but from his own body and sense of self.

"I feel like I've been holding myself together, but I'm starting to crack," Mark admitted. "I want to feel like I'm more than just his partner. I want to feel like I'm wanted, like I'm needed—physically, emotionally. I just don't know how to talk to him about it without making him feel like he's doing something wrong."

This was the heart of Mark's struggle: the fear of speaking up and potentially making his boyfriend feel inadequate. It's so common, especially among men, to fear that asking for affection or touch might be seen as weak or needy, or worse, as a criticism of their partner's love. Mark was caught between wanting something more—something that was integral to his emotional health—and not wanting to make his boyfriend feel like he was falling short.

But the truth is, everyone has different needs when it comes to intimacy. It's not about someone being wrong or not trying enough; it's about understanding how we give and receive love. And it's perfectly okay to need something that your partner might not immediately understand. The challenge lies in communicating that need in a way that doesn't place blame but invites both partners into a conversation about how to meet each other's emotional and physical needs.

The Struggle of Feeling Alone in a Relationship

Mark's situation is one I've seen more often than you might think. So many people enter relationships with expectations that their emotional and physical needs will be naturally met because they love each other. And in many cases, that's true. But when touch is at the core of one partner's emotional needs, and the other doesn't understand or doesn't share that same need, it can create a silent, unseen gap between them.

Mark wasn't asking for anything extravagant. He wasn't demanding constant affection, or looking for romantic gestures every day. He simply wanted to be held sometimes. He wanted to curl up on the couch with his boyfriend and feel the warmth of his body, without the pressure of sex or an agenda. He wanted to know that he was desired not just for the person he was, but for the physical presence he brought into the relationship.

"I feel like I'm always the one initiating everything," he said. "I try to touch him when we're sitting together, but it never feels like enough. It feels like I'm just doing it to get something, not like he wants it too."

And this is where Mark's true emotional need was coming from: the desire to feel like his touch was wanted in return, not just given in a way that felt one-sided or transactional. He needed to know that his physical affection had value beyond what it could lead to. It wasn't just about the connection—it was about the warmth and reassurance that came with that closeness.

Helping Mark Communicate His Need

We spent some time exploring how Mark could have that conversation with his boyfriend. I encouraged him to frame it as a positive expression of his desire for a deeper connection, rather than as a complaint or a criticism. He needed to find a way to express how important touch was to him—not in a way that placed blame, but in a way that invited his boyfriend to see and hear him.

"I think I've been holding it in because I'm afraid of making him feel bad," Mark admitted. "I don't want him to think he's not good enough. I just want to feel like he really wants to be with me in that way."

I reminded him that expressing his needs wasn't about criticizing his partner—it was about strengthening their relationship. By sharing his needs openly, he wasn't just asking for physical affection. He was asking for the vulnerability that came with it—the shared intimacy that can only come from truly being seen and touched in ways that speak to the soul.

Mark eventually found the courage to have that conversation. It wasn't easy, and it took time. But when he finally opened up to his boyfriend about his need for touch and physical closeness, his boyfriend was receptive. He admitted that he had always struggled with expressing affection, but that he loved Mark deeply and wanted to make him feel valued in every way. They worked together to find new ways to share affection, to incorporate touch into their daily life, even in small ways—whether it was holding hands on a walk, a longer hug after a long day, or simply sitting close on the couch without expectation.

The Takeaway: Understanding and Communicating Your Needs

Mark's journey wasn't about finding someone new or seeking out something he couldn't get in his relationship. It was about realizing that his need for touch was an essential part of who he was, and that sharing that need wasn't a weakness, but an invitation for his partner to understand him more deeply. It was about creating space for his boyfriend to learn and grow alongside him.

If there's one thing I want you to take away from Mark's story, it's this: it's okay to ask for what you need. It's okay to be vulnerable. And it's okay to have needs that your partner may not initially understand, as long as you communicate them with love and care. Relationships are built on mutual understanding, and often, it's the conversations that feel uncomfortable at first that lead to the most profound shifts.

You deserve to feel wanted, desired, and connected—not just emotionally, but physically. And sometimes, it's a simple touch, a lingering hug, or a moment of closeness that can make all the difference in the world.

Chapter 10: Reaching Across Time

He walked into the room with a quiet dignity, his movements slow but deliberate. There was a gentleness about him that immediately caught my attention. William was in his late 70s, neatly dressed in a pressed shirt and slacks, the kind of man who carried himself with the air of someone who had seen and lived through much. But behind his composed exterior, I could sense a profound loneliness, like an unspoken weight he carried with him.

As we sat down to talk before the session, William's words came hesitantly at first, like a faucet slowly releasing water after being closed tightly for too long. "I've been on my own for quite a while now," he said, his voice calm but tinged with sadness. "My wife passed away ten years ago, and my friends... well, let's just say they're not as easy to find these days."

William's story wasn't unusual, but that didn't make it any less poignant. He had spent decades building a life with his wife, raising children, working hard, and cherishing their time together. But after her passing, and with his children now living their own busy lives far away, he found himself in a house that once felt full of love but now echoed with silence.

The Quiet Loneliness of Growing Older

As he shared more, William admitted something that struck me deeply: "I don't think I've been touched in years—not really, anyway. My kids hug me when they visit, but that's maybe once or twice a year. And the rest of the time... well, there's no one."

Touch. Such a simple, basic human need, yet one that often becomes scarce as people grow older. William's experience wasn't just about the loss of his wife; it was about the loss of physical connection, the small, everyday gestures that remind us we are alive and that we matter to someone else. A hand on the shoulder, a hug at the end of the day, even the casual brushing of fingers when passing someone something—these were all things William hadn't experienced in years.

"I feel invisible sometimes," he admitted, looking down at his hands. "I go out to the store, I see people on the street, but it's like I'm just a ghost walking through. No one really sees me. And no one touches me. It's like I'm not there."

That sentence stayed with me long after William left our first session. "No one touches me." It's such a powerful reminder of how deeply intertwined touch is with our sense of self-worth and existence. For William, it wasn't just about physical affection—it was about being acknowledged, being reminded that he still had value, that he was still deserving of connection.

Rediscovering Dignity Through Touch

In our first session together, I could see the hesitation in William's posture. When I invited him to lie down on the massage table, he paused for a moment before finally settling himself, almost as if he were bracing for the unfamiliarity of being touched. I reassured him with my voice, explaining each step before I began.

"I want this to be a space where you can simply be," I told him. "There's no expectation, no rush. This is about giving you the connection you deserve."

As I placed my hands gently on his shoulders to begin, I felt the tension in his body. It was as if years of carrying the weight of grief and isolation had settled into his muscles. Slowly, as the session went on, I could feel him begin to relax. His breathing deepened, and the rigidity in his shoulders softened. I worked with intention, focusing on creating a safe and nurturing space for him to simply exist and be cared for.

When the session ended, William sat up and took a deep breath. His eyes were watery but kind. "I didn't realize how much I missed this," he said quietly. "It's not just the touch itself. It's... it's feeling like I matter again. Like someone sees me."

The Transformative Power of Connection

Over the weeks that followed, William returned for more sessions. With each visit, I noticed subtle changes in him. His posture improved, his movements became more fluid, and he started sharing stories about his life—about his wife, his children, and the adventures he'd had in his younger years. It was as if, through touch and connection, he was rediscovering parts of himself he had buried under the weight of loneliness.

One day, he told me about a recent trip to the park. "I've started going more often," he said, smiling. "I sit on a bench, and sometimes people stop to chat. It's nice, you know? To feel like I'm part of the world again."

What struck me most about William's journey was how touch wasn't just healing his loneliness—it was restoring his sense of dignity. It reminded him that he was worthy of care, of attention, of affection. It reminded him that his existence mattered, not just to those who had known him in the past, but to the world around him now.

A Lesson for All of Us

William's story is one of many, but it carries an important message: no one should have to go through life feeling invisible or untouched. And yet, for so many older men, this is their reality. They are seen as strong, self-reliant, or simply "fine" because they don't often voice their need for connection. But underneath that exterior, there is often a longing to be seen, to be acknowledged, to be touched.

Touch isn't just about physical contact—it's about connection, about saying, "I see you. You are here, and you matter." For men like William, it's a lifeline, a way to rediscover themselves and reclaim their place in a world that sometimes feels like it has moved on without them.

As I reflect on William's journey, I am reminded of why this work is so important. It's not just about providing comfort or relief in the moment. It's about helping people remember their worth, their humanity, and their capacity for connection—no matter their age or stage of life. And it's about creating a space where they can feel truly, deeply seen.

Chapter 11: The Strain of Success

From the moment Jason walked into my space, I could see why people would describe him as "intimidating." He was tall, impeccably dressed in a tailored suit, and carried himself with the confidence of someone who was used to running the show. His handshake was firm, his posture upright, and his expression unreadable. He looked every inch the high-powered executive he was—poised, polished, and in control.

But as he sat down across from me and loosened his tie, I noticed the slightest flicker of something beneath the surface—something raw and unguarded, a glimpse of the human being behind the polished exterior.

"I've never done anything like this before," Jason admitted, his tone somewhere between skeptical and hopeful. "Honestly, I'm not even sure why I'm here. But I... I just feel like I need something."

The Weight of Perfection

Jason went on to explain his life: a career in finance that had skyrocketed him to the top, a sprawling corner office, international travel, and a lifestyle most people could only dream of. He had the house, the car, the accolades. Yet despite all of it, he confessed, "I feel like I'm running on fumes. Everyone looks to me for answers, for leadership, for solutions, but... who do I turn to? I don't even know how to ask for what I need."

As he spoke, I could hear the exhaustion in his voice, see the tension etched into his face. Jason wasn't just tired from the demands of his job—he was tired from the constant performance, the need to project strength and competence every second of every day.

He described a world where vulnerability was seen as weakness, where even admitting to needing something as basic as touch or connection felt like failing. "I've built this image of myself," he said, "and I don't know how to be anything else. But lately, I just feel... empty. Disconnected. Like I'm living someone else's life."

Breaking Down the Armor

As we began our session, Jason carried that same guarded energy onto the tatami mat. His body was stiff, his breathing shallow, and even in a space designed for relaxation, he seemed to be bracing himself. I worked slowly, using light, grounding touches to help him ease into the experience.

"Jason," I said gently, "you don't have to be anything here. Not a leader, not an executive, not in control. This is a space where you can just... be."

I could see the words sink in, but it took time for his body to follow suit. Bit by bit, as I continued to work, I noticed the tightness in his shoulders begin to soften, his breathing grow deeper. It wasn't until midway through the session that I felt the full shift—a moment when his body finally let go, as if surrendering to the idea that it was okay to let someone else hold the weight for a while.

At the end of the session, Jason sat up slowly, his expression softer than it had been when he arrived. "That was... different," he said, searching for the right words. "I didn't realize how much I needed this. Just... to let go."

The Pressure to Be Perfect

In the weeks that followed, Jason and I continued to work together. Each session brought new layers of insight and release. One day, he shared something that stuck with me.

"Do you know how often I hear people say, 'You're so lucky' or 'You have it all figured out'?" he said. "It's like they see this version of me that I barely recognize anymore. But I feel like I can't tell anyone that. I'm supposed to be the guy who has it all together."

Jason's story is one I've heard in different forms from many men who come to see me—men who have achieved outward success but feel an inner emptiness they don't know how to address. For Jason, the biggest challenge wasn't the external demands of his career; it was the internal conflict between the image he had built and the vulnerability he so desperately needed.

Finding Strength in Vulnerability

Through our sessions, Jason began to see that vulnerability wasn't a weakness but a strength. It wasn't about falling apart or losing control—it was about acknowledging his humanity and allowing himself to feel.

One day, he told me, "I realized something the other night. I've been so focused on what I think people expect from me that I've stopped asking myself what I need. For years, I've been running on autopilot, and this... this has been like hitting the reset button."

Jason started making changes in his life—small ones at first, like taking a day off to spend time hiking or calling a friend he hadn't spoken to in years. But those small changes began to add up. He started prioritizing his well-being in ways he hadn't allowed himself to before.

"I'm learning to let people in," he said during one session. "It's not easy, and I'm still figuring it out, but I'm starting to see that being strong doesn't mean carrying everything alone. Sometimes strength is letting someone else help you carry the load."

A Lesson for All of Us

Jason's journey reminded me of something I wish every man could hear: you don't have to do it all alone. Society often tells men that their value lies in their ability to provide, to lead, to protect—but it doesn't often make space for their need to be cared for in return.

For men like Jason, professional intimacy becomes a lifeline—a place where they can shed the expectations of the world and simply be themselves. It's not about fixing them or solving their problems. It's about creating a space where they can reconnect with their humanity, their vulnerability, and their strength.

Because at the end of the day, we all need connection. We all need to be seen, to be touched, to be reminded that we're not alone. And for men like Jason, who carry the weight of the world on their shoulders, that reminder can be life-changing.

Chapter 12: Reclaiming the Pieces

Some men walk into my space with an air of quiet strength. Others enter cautiously, their body language guarded, as though bracing for a storm that hasn't arrived. When Sam arrived for his first session, he was different. There was a weight in his presence, something that spoke not of strength or fear, but of exhaustion—the kind that comes from carrying pain alone for too long.

Sam was a survivor of trauma, though he didn't use that word to describe himself at first. He introduced himself as someone "just looking to feel normal again." He spoke hesitantly, choosing his words carefully, as if unsure what was safe to share.

"I've been through some... stuff," he said. "It's in the past, but I can't seem to leave it there. I thought I could move on, but I don't even know what that means anymore."

Carrying the Scars

As Sam began to share more about his story, it became clear just how deeply his experiences had shaped him. He had survived abuse, though he downplayed the severity of it. "It wasn't that bad," he said, his voice flat, even as his body told a different story. His shoulders hunched protectively, and his hands fidgeted restlessly in his lap.

Over time, he revealed how his past had left him with a fractured sense of self. He struggled to trust others, to let his guard down, even in relationships where he knew intellectually that he was safe. And then there was his relationship with touch.

"It's weird," he said during one session. "I crave it, but I'm also terrified of it. Sometimes, just the thought of someone touching me makes my skin crawl. But at the same time... I miss it. I miss feeling close to someone, feeling connected."

The Challenge of Rebuilding Trust

Working with Sam required a level of care and patience that went beyond the physical. Trauma often leaves behind not just emotional wounds but also physical memories. The body holds on to pain, fear, and tension in ways that words alone can't always address.

When Sam first came to see me, even the idea of touch was overwhelming. We spent our early sessions focused solely on creating a sense of safety. I let him set the pace, always asking for his consent and reassuring him that he was in control.

"Tell me what feels okay and what doesn't," I told him. "This is your space, and nothing happens here without your permission."

We started with something as simple as placing a hand on his arm, letting him get used to the sensation of touch in a safe and controlled environment. It was a slow process, but with each session, I could see him beginning to relax, his body learning to distinguish between danger and safety.

The Power of Safe Touch

One day, during a session, Sam said something that stuck with me. "I didn't realize how much I needed this—not just the touch, but the choice. The freedom to say yes or no and know that it's okay either way."

That's the thing about trauma—it often robs people of their sense of agency. For Sam, our sessions weren't just about experiencing touch; they were about reclaiming his autonomy, learning that he could set boundaries and still be cared for.

As we worked together, Sam began to rediscover what touch could feel like when it wasn't tied to pain or fear. He described it as a kind of reawakening, a way of reconnecting with a part of himself he thought he had lost.

Healing Is a Journey

Sam's healing journey wasn't linear—few are. There were days when he felt like he had made progress, and others when old fears crept back in. But over time, he began to notice the changes. He started holding his head higher, his posture less guarded. He began opening up more, sharing stories about his hobbies, his friends, his hopes for the future.

One day, toward the end of a session, he said, "For the first time in years, I feel… lighter. Like I'm not carrying all of it by myself anymore."

Those words hit me deeply because they captured what I hope every man who walks into my space takes away: the understanding that they don't have to carry their pain alone, that it's okay to ask for help, and that healing is possible—even after the darkest experiences.

What Trauma Teaches Us About Connection

Working with men like Sam has taught me so much about the resilience of the human spirit. Trauma can shatter a person's sense of self, but it doesn't have to define them. With the right support, people can heal, rebuild, and rediscover the joy of connection.

For many men, though, asking for that support is the hardest step. Society often tells men that strength means suppressing their pain, that seeking help is a sign of weakness. But in reality, the courage it takes to face one's trauma, to open up and allow someone else to help carry the load—that is strength in its truest form.

Sam's journey reminded me of the incredible power of touch, not just as a physical experience but as a deeply emotional one. Touch has the ability to say what words can't: You are safe. You are cared for. You are not alone.

And for men like Sam, who have spent years feeling isolated and unseen, those messages can be profoundly healing. Because at the end of the day, we all need to feel connected—not just to others, but to ourselves.

Chapter 13: Redefining the Mirror

I remember the first time James reached out to me. He was in his early 50s, and his voice trembled a bit as he explained why he was contacting me. He spoke of a quiet confusion, something that had been simmering for years, maybe even decades—an unease that he could never quite name but always felt in his gut. He described a life full of personal achievements, a loving family, and a career he had worked tirelessly to build. Yet, there was an unspoken weight, a tension between who he was expected to be and who he felt himself to be deep down. He was struggling with his identity— in terms of sexuality — and it was creating an internal conflict that seemed to seep into all areas of his life.

"I know I'm supposed to be happy with the life I've built," James told me, "But something feels off. I don't know what's missing, but I do know that I'm tired of pretending that I'm okay. I'm not sure who I really am anymore."

The Challenge Of Conforming

James had always followed the traditional paths laid out before him—getting married, having children, doing the things society told him were right for a man. But as he entered his 50s, he began questioning if those paths had been his to follow, or if they were ones he had walked simply because that's what was expected of him. He had never felt fully comfortable with his own body and the labels that had been assigned to him, labels like "straight," "husband," and "father." Deep down, he wondered if there was more to him, something he hadn't been able to fully express or even understand.

This kind of internal questioning, especially at a time when society still holds such rigid ideas about gender roles and sexuality, can be an incredibly isolating experience. I could hear the quiet sense of shame in his voice as he spoke about his longing for touch and intimacy but his fear of being judged or misunderstood. He wasn't just wrestling with external expectations; he was also grappling with the emotional and physical needs he had been taught to suppress. He wanted to explore his desires, to find comfort in his body, and to experience touch without shame or fear. But the confusion he felt about his own sexual identity made it difficult to know where to begin.

Confronting Shame

When he came to see me for our first session, I could sense that he was carrying years of self-doubt with him. He didn't know where his journey would lead, but he knew it was time to start unraveling the pieces of himself that had been tucked away for far too long. The space we created together was one of non-judgmental acceptance—a place where he could be exactly who he was without fear of societal labels. He shared that, for the first time in a long time, he felt like he could explore his feelings without the pressure to conform to anyone else's expectations.

Our sessions focused not just on his physical touch needs, but also on the emotional work of self-discovery. Touch, for James, was something he had not truly allowed himself to experience in years. It had always been intertwined with the expectations of heterosexual intimacy, or limited to quick moments with his wife. But now, as he explored his identity more deeply, he began to see that touch didn't have to be tied to any label. It didn't have to be sexual, nor did it have to be defined by society's narrow expectations of what a man's touch should look like.

Through our time together, James began to unearth the layers of shame and confusion that had built up over the years. He started to realize that his desires for touch, connection, and emotional intimacy were valid, no matter what form they took. Whether it was a simple touch on the arm, a comforting hug, or the more vulnerable acts of physical closeness, he began to embrace the fact that his need for touch was just as natural as anyone else's. It didn't make him any less of a man, nor did it dictate his sexuality or gender.

One Size Doesn't Fit All

We also spent time discussing the concept of gender fluidity and how many people experience their gender on a spectrum. For James, this was a revelation. He had always felt like he had to fit neatly into one box or another, but over time, he began to see that he didn't need to label himself in such a rigid way. His understanding of masculinity evolved, and he saw that masculinity, like sexuality, is not one-size-fits-all. It's dynamic, fluid, and can be expressed in many different ways. The more he accepted his own complexity, the more at peace he became with the contradictions he felt inside.

In a particularly memorable session, James talked about a time when he had attended a yoga retreat with his wife. During a partner yoga session, he was paired with another man. As they did poses that required physical closeness, he found himself feeling both uncomfortable and deeply relaxed at the same time. The touch wasn't sexual—it was purely supportive, affirming, and rooted in trust. For the first time in his life, he understood what it felt like to receive touch without any expectation of it turning into something more. It wasn't about sex; it was about presence, mutual respect, and connection. That moment marked a turning point for James, where he realized that his need for touch didn't have to be tied to a specific gender or sexual orientation. He could experience meaningful touch without shame, guilt, or the need to label it.

Permission Granted

Through his journey, James learned to give himself permission to explore his identity on his own terms. His relationship with his body, and with others, transformed. He began to look at touch not just as an intimate act, but as a powerful form of communication—one that transcends words, expectations, and labels. In doing so, he learned to honor his own needs, not as a way of fitting into a societal mold, but as a way of truly honoring who he was at his core.

At the end of our work together, James expressed a deep sense of relief. "I feel like I'm finally allowed to just be myself," he said. "I've spent so many years feeling like I had to hide parts of me. But now, I understand that my journey is my own—and it's okay to embrace all of it, without fear."

His story is one of many that illustrates how, as men, we are often told to suppress parts of ourselves that don't fit the societal mold of what it means to be a man. But the truth is, embracing the fullness of who we are, without shame or fear, is one of the most liberating acts we can make. Whether it's exploring our identity, our desire for touch, or simply our emotional needs, there is power in breaking free from the labels that society has placed on us.

James' journey shows us that it's never too late to explore who we are, to reconnect with our bodies, and to experience touch as a form of love, connection, and self-affirmation. The work of self-discovery is ongoing, and the space we create to explore those questions is an essential part of healing and growth. It's time to give ourselves permission to be whole and complete in all the ways that we are—without fear, shame, or limitation.

Chapter 14: The Courage to Be Both

I first met Jake in his late 20s, a man who seemed like he had everything figured out on the outside. He had a solid job, a great group of friends, and a charming, confident demeanor that people often admired. But despite all that, something inside of him felt deeply out of sync. He struggled with his identity as a man, unsure of what it really meant to be masculine in a world where expectations were often so rigid and contradictory. He felt disconnected from his own sense of self, constantly battling internalized shame about his emotional needs and vulnerability.

A Struggle with Societal Expectations

When Jake first came to see me, he told me he felt like he was living in a box that society had built for him—a box labeled "what it means to be a man." He described how, from a young age, he had been taught that men had to be strong, stoic, and independent. Showing any kind of emotion, let alone expressing vulnerability, was seen as weakness in his world. For Jake, even the simplest desire for connection or affection was something he had learned to bury deep inside.

"I feel like I'm constantly walking around with this emotional armor," he said. "I have these feelings, but I don't know what to do with them. It feels wrong to express them."

Jake's internal struggle was not unique. Many men grow up with the belief that their masculinity is defined by how little they need others, especially when it comes to emotional support or physical connection. Showing any softness or sensitivity is often seen as incompatible with being a "real" man. Over time, Jake had internalized these messages, which made it nearly impossible for him to reconcile his need for touch, affection, and emotional depth with the image of masculinity he had always aspired to.

Breaking Down the Armor

In our first few sessions, we began to explore what it would mean for Jake to embrace both his strength and his vulnerability. I explained that being a man didn't mean abandoning his emotional needs or ignoring the desire for connection; instead, those qualities were a crucial part of being a whole and authentic man. I reminded him that masculinity, like anything else, is not one-size-fits-all. There's no single definition of what it means to be masculine, and true strength often comes from being able to embrace and express all aspects of ourselves—emotionally, physically, and mentally.

Our work together focused on breaking down the "armor" Jake had built up around himself over the years. The emotional walls he had erected in order to protect himself from judgment or perceived weakness had only kept him disconnected from others—and from himself. We talked about how these walls weren't just holding back his emotional vulnerability; they were also limiting his ability to experience the deeper connections he longed for. He began to see that allowing himself to be vulnerable didn't diminish his masculinity; in fact, it made him more human, more authentic, and more capable of forming meaningful relationships.

The Power of Touch and Connection

One of the most powerful breakthroughs for Jake came when we began to explore the role of touch in emotional connection. For a long time, he had viewed physical touch as something to be earned or reserved for certain moments of intimacy. It was either a casual handshake or a hug between friends, but he never allowed himself to experience the healing power of touch in a deeper, more nurturing way. He believed that touch was only for romantic or sexual contexts, and that needing or seeking it outside of those situations would somehow make him less of a man.

Through our sessions, I encouraged Jake to explore how different types of touch could help him reconnect with his own emotions and with others in a healthy way. I taught him that touch isn't just about intimacy; it's about presence, comfort, and the mutual exchange of care. I helped him understand that receiving and giving touch—whether it's a hand on the shoulder, a firm handshake, or even a friendly hug—can be an empowering act for men, one that reaffirms our humanity and our ability to give and receive support.

At first, Jake was hesitant. The idea of seeking or accepting touch outside of a romantic context felt foreign to him, even uncomfortable. But over time, he began to experiment with touch in more platonic and nurturing ways. He allowed himself to receive a hug from a close friend without feeling ashamed. He practiced simple self-touch, like rubbing his own shoulders after a long day, acknowledging his body and its needs. As he experienced the physical sensation of touch in these ways, Jake began to feel something shift inside of him—a quiet, profound sense of relief and connectedness.

Embracing Both Strength and Vulnerability

As Jake began to open up to touch, we also worked on exploring his emotional vulnerability. He realized that by allowing himself to be soft and vulnerable, he wasn't losing his strength; he was actually embracing it. Emotional vulnerability is not a sign of weakness, but rather an indication of emotional maturity and strength. When men allow themselves to be open about their emotions, they empower themselves and others to do the same. Jake began to recognize that expressing his feelings—whether it was about work stress, relationship issues, or personal struggles—was not only healthy but also an essential part of being a complete and whole man.

In one particularly revealing session, Jake shared how, for the first time, he had opened up to his father about his struggles with identity and masculinity. To his surprise, his father responded with compassion and understanding, instead of the judgment or dismissal Jake had feared. That moment of vulnerability created a bridge between them, allowing their relationship to deepen and grow. Jake realized that vulnerability, rather than isolating him, had actually brought him closer to the people he cared about.

A New Understanding of Masculinity

By the end of our work together, Jake had begun to redefine what masculinity meant for him. He no longer felt that his emotional needs were in conflict with his identity as a man. Instead, he saw that his strength was enhanced by his willingness to embrace both his vulnerability and his need for connection. Masculinity, for Jake, was no longer about meeting societal expectations of toughness or emotional detachment. It was about being authentic, present, and open —both with himself and with others.

Jake's journey serves as a powerful reminder that masculinity is not a static set of traits but a dynamic, evolving expression of who we are. It's time for men to realize that strength is not about bottling up emotions or avoiding vulnerability—it's about the courage to be whole, to embrace all aspects of ourselves, and to be unapologetic in our need for connection.

Through touch, vulnerability, and emotional openness, men can reconnect with their true selves and live more authentic, fulfilling lives. Jake's story is a testament to the power of this journey, and to the transformative effect that embracing both strength and vulnerability can have on a man's life.

Chapter 15: The Quiet Weight of Loss

When I first met David, he walked into the room with a calm, composed demeanor. He was in his late sixties, neatly dressed, and carried himself with a kind of quiet self-assurance. There was a warmth in his smile, and his handshake was firm but gentle. As we sat down, he spoke with an air of self-awareness, even humor, about how he'd never done anything like this before. "I'm curious," he said, "but I think I just want to see what it feels like to be held."

David seemed cheerful, even relaxed, as we talked. There was no hint of the storm that was brewing just beneath the surface. He didn't mention his loss or the weight of his grief—at least, not then.

The Tears That Came Unbidden

When we moved into the cuddle, I could feel the tension in his body. It wasn't unusual; many people come into this space with a mix of anticipation and nervousness. But as we settled into a comfortable position—his head resting lightly against my shoulder, my arms around him—something shifted almost immediately.

His body softened for a moment, and then, without warning, he began to sob.

At first, it was a quiet, trembling kind of crying, but it quickly grew into deep, gut-wrenching sobs. His whole body shook as years of unspoken grief and unexpressed emotion came pouring out. I held him gently, not saying a word, just being there for him, creating a safe space for him to let it all out.

For more than 20 minutes, he cried. He apologized several times, in between sobs, his voice breaking with shame and vulnerability. Each time, I reassured him, "You have nothing to apologize for. Let it out. This is your space."

I could feel the weight of his grief as though it were something tangible in the room. It was a sacred moment, one of those times when you realize how much pain people carry silently, hidden behind polite smiles and brave faces.

His Story Unfolds

When the sobbing finally began to subside, David took a deep, shaky breath. "I'm sorry," he said again, wiping his face with trembling hands.

"You don't have to be," I said softly. "You've been holding this for a long time, haven't you?"

He nodded, and then, in a voice tinged with both relief and sorrow, he began to tell me his story.

David had been married to his wife, Helen, for 34 years. She was, as he described her, "the love of my life, my best friend, my everything." They had built a life together, raising children, traveling, and sharing the small, beautiful moments that make up a marriage.

Four years ago, Helen passed away after a brief illness. "She was gone so quickly," he said, his voice breaking. "One moment we were planning our next trip, and the next, I was planning her funeral."

Since her passing, David had thrown himself into staying busy—volunteering, spending time with his grandchildren, keeping up appearances. But there was one thing he hadn't allowed himself to acknowledge: the absence of touch.

"For 34 years, I always had her," he said. "Her hand on my shoulder, her arms around me, the way she'd lean into me when we sat on the couch. And then... nothing. I didn't realize how much I missed it until I couldn't take it anymore."

The Power of Being Held

David's story stayed with me long after our session ended. It was a poignant reminder of how much we, as humans, need touch—not just as a physical act, but as a way to feel connected, seen, and loved.

For David, the act of being held wasn't just about comfort; it was about releasing years of grief that he had carried silently. It was about giving himself permission to be vulnerable, to let go of the stoicism he had clung to for so long.

Touch has a way of unlocking emotions we didn't even know we were holding. It creates a space where words aren't necessary, where the body can express what the heart has been carrying.

A Lesson in Vulnerability

David's journey reminded me of the courage it takes to seek connection, especially after loss. It's not easy to admit that we need something as simple—and as profound—as touch. Society often tells us to "be strong," to push through our pain without leaning on others. But strength isn't about holding everything in; it's about knowing when to let it out.

When David left that day, he looked lighter, as though the weight he had been carrying had shifted, even if just a little. He smiled at me—a genuine, heartfelt smile—and said, "Thank you. I didn't know how much I needed this."

It was a reminder to me, too, of why this work matters. In a world that often overlooks the power of touch, creating a space for people like David to feel seen, held, and understood is a gift I'm honored to give.

David's story is one of loss, yes, but also of healing. It's a testament to the resilience of the human spirit and the profound impact of something as simple as being held.

Part 3: The Unique Challenges Men Face

"Connection is why we're here; it is what gives purpose and meaning to our lives."

— Brené Brown

Chapter 16: Breaking Through the Shame

When I first met Gerald, he was visibly nervous. He shifted in his chair, avoiding eye contact, and his hands fidgeted in his lap. "I never thought I'd actually do this," he admitted. "I mean... coming to someone for touch? It feels so... weird. Like, what's wrong with me that I need this?"

Gerald wasn't the first man to walk into my practice carrying a heavy load of shame, and he certainly wouldn't be the last. It's a story I hear again and again—men struggling with the deeply ingrained belief that needing care, connection, or touch is a sign of weakness.

The Weight of Societal Stigma

In our culture, the idea of men seeking professional intimacy services often sparks misunderstanding, if not outright judgment. There's a pervasive stigma around touch, particularly when it's sought outside the confines of traditional relationships.

For many men, the shame begins long before they even consider stepping into a space like mine. From a young age, they're taught that independence and self-reliance are the hallmarks of masculinity. Vulnerability, on the other hand, is seen as a flaw—a crack in the armor.

And yet, the need for touch and connection is universal. We're wired for it. Denying that need doesn't make it disappear; it just buries it deeper, where it festers into loneliness, anxiety, or even physical pain.

Gerald had spent years battling that inner conflict. On the surface, he had a great life—a steady job, good friends, a comfortable home. But beneath it all, there was an ache he couldn't quite name.

The Shame of Admitting a Need

When Gerald first reached out, he was hesitant to explain why. "I don't even know if this is the right thing for me," he said. "I just... I feel like there's something missing. But it's embarrassing, you know? Like, I should be able to figure this out on my own."

That word—embarrassing—came up a lot during our early conversations. Gerald worried about what others would think if they found out. He worried about what he thought of himself.

"I mean, isn't this the kind of thing people go to when they're desperate?" he asked one day, his voice tinged with self-deprecation.

"No," I told him gently. "This is the kind of thing people go to when they're brave enough to admit they want more for themselves."

A Journey Toward Vulnerability

It took time for Gerald to feel comfortable in our sessions. At first, he seemed hyper-aware of everything— where my hands were, how he was breathing, whether he was "doing it right." It was as if he expected to be judged or found lacking.

But as the sessions continued, something began to shift. Gerald started to relax, his body softening as he allowed himself to simply be. One day, after a particularly quiet session, he said, "I didn't realize how much I was holding in. It's like... I've been clenching my whole life, and I didn't even know it."

For Gerald, the sessions weren't just about the touch itself. They were about unlearning the shame he had internalized, about giving himself permission to receive care without judgment.

Overcoming the Stigma

One of the most powerful moments came when Gerald finally opened up about why he had come to see me. "I've always felt like I'm not allowed to need anything," he said. "Like, I'm supposed to have it all together, all the time. But the truth is, I don't. I don't always have it together. And I think... I think I'm finally okay with that."

Hearing those words was a reminder of why I do this work. For so many men, the hardest part isn't the first session—it's getting to the point where they believe they deserve it.

Gerald's journey was about more than breaking through his own shame; it was about reclaiming his humanity. He realized that needing touch, care, and connection doesn't make him weak—it makes him human.

The Courage to Seek Connection

By the end of our time together, Gerald had a newfound sense of confidence, not just in himself but in his ability to embrace vulnerability. "This isn't something I ever thought I'd do," he said during our final session. "But I'm so glad I did. It's like I've been walking around with blinders on, and now I can finally see what I've been missing."

Stories like Gerald's remind me that breaking through shame isn't a one-time event; it's a process. It takes courage to confront the messages we've been told about who we're supposed to be and what we're allowed to feel. But when men take that step, the transformation can be profound.

I often think about how different the world could be if we didn't burden men with the stigma of seeking care. What if we taught boys that it's okay to ask for help, that needing connection isn't a flaw but a strength?

Gerald's story, like so many others, is a testament to the power of vulnerability. It's a reminder that shame loses its grip when we shine a light on it, when we speak our needs aloud and allow ourselves to be seen.

Because at the end of the day, seeking connection isn't something to be ashamed of—it's something to celebrate.

Chapter 17: Masculinity and Intimacy

When Derek walked into my space for the first time, I could sense the weight he carried. He was tall, broad-shouldered, with a commanding presence that seemed to fill the room. He gave a firm handshake, his posture stiff, his face carefully neutral. "I don't even know why I'm here," he said, his voice measured. "I guess I just... something feels off, and I thought maybe you could help."

This wasn't unusual. Men like Derek often show up uncertain, guarded, and deeply conditioned by a lifetime of cultural messages about what it means to "be a man." For Derek, and many others like him, masculinity had become a kind of armor—protective, yes, but also isolating.

The Cultural Cage of Masculinity

Our culture often equates masculinity with stoicism, strength, and independence. From a young age, boys are taught to "man up," to hide their tears, to avoid appearing too emotional, lest they risk being seen as weak.

These messages are subtle but pervasive. They seep into every corner of a man's life, shaping how he relates to himself and others. Vulnerability becomes a liability. Intimacy, both emotional and physical, is carefully rationed, often reserved only for romantic partners—if at all.

For many men, the idea of openly expressing emotions feels foreign, even dangerous. Instead, they bottle up their feelings, channeling them into work, hobbies, or silent endurance. This "emotional armoring" might protect them in the short term, but over time, it takes a toll—on their relationships, their mental health, and their ability to connect.

Dismantling Emotional Armor

In our first session, Derek was polite but distant. His responses were clipped, his body language tense. When I asked what brought him here, he hesitated before saying, "I don't really do emotions. My wife says I'm... closed off. But I've been like this my whole life. I don't know how to change it."

That's the tricky thing about emotional armor—it feels so natural, so necessary, that it becomes part of a man's identity. Letting go of it can feel like losing a piece of yourself.

But healing doesn't happen by force. It happens through patience, trust, and small, consistent steps. For Derek, that meant creating a space where he could explore vulnerability without fear of judgment or rejection.

The Power of Safe Space

Our sessions weren't just about touch—they were about helping Derek reconnect with the parts of himself he had buried. Early on, I could see how much he struggled to relax. His muscles were tense, his breathing shallow. "I'm not used to this," he admitted. "It feels... weird to just sit and not have to do anything."

I reassured him that this discomfort was normal, a sign that he was stepping outside his comfort zone. Slowly, as we worked together, Derek began to soften. He allowed himself to experience the simple, profound act of being cared for.

One day, after a particularly quiet session, he opened his eyes and said, "I didn't realize how much I've been holding in. It's like I've been carrying this weight, and I didn't even know it was there."

Redefining Masculinity

As Derek's emotional armor began to crack, he started to see masculinity in a new light. "I used to think being strong meant not showing any weakness," he said during one of our conversations. "But now I'm starting to think... maybe real strength is being able to open up. To let people in."

This shift didn't happen overnight, but it was profound. Derek began to realize that masculinity doesn't have to be a cage. It can be flexible, expansive, and deeply connected.

By the end of our time together, Derek had transformed his understanding of himself and his relationships. He started having deeper conversations with his wife, sharing feelings he had long kept hidden. He allowed himself to cry in front of her for the first time in years, and instead of feeling ashamed, he felt free.

The Journey to Authentic Connection

Derek's story is a reminder that intimacy and masculinity aren't opposites—they can coexist beautifully. But getting there requires dismantling the cultural narratives that keep men locked in emotional isolation.

Through my work, I've seen countless men like Derek rediscover parts of themselves they thought were lost. They learn that vulnerability isn't weakness; it's courage. That asking for help doesn't diminish their masculinity; it strengthens it.

What if we taught boys that strength isn't about suppressing emotions but embracing them? What if we showed men that intimacy—whether it's through touch, conversation, or shared experiences—isn't something to fear but something to celebrate?

Breaking through emotional armor isn't easy. It takes time, trust, and a willingness to face discomfort. But when men like Derek take that step, they often find that what lies beneath isn't weakness—it's strength, connection, and a deeper sense of self.

Masculinity doesn't have to be a lonely journey. It can be a rich, rewarding experience of love, care, and authenticity. And it starts with letting go of the armor.

On Being Seen

Chapter 18: The Role of Consent and Boundaries for Men

I'll never forget the conversation I had with a client named Ryan during our first session. He sat across from me, fidgeting with his hands, and said, "I know this might sound strange, but... I'm not really sure what boundaries even feel like. I mean, I know what the word means, but growing up, no one ever really talked about it. And now, I think I've gotten it wrong more times than I'd like to admit."

Ryan's honesty struck a chord with me because he's far from alone in this struggle. Many men come to my sessions carrying a similar uncertainty—not because they're inherently careless or disrespectful, but because they've never been given the tools to understand or navigate boundaries.

For generations, our culture has sent men conflicting messages about touch, intimacy, and connection. They've been told to take charge, to be assertive, to never show weakness. But they've rarely been taught how to ask, listen, and negotiate—the cornerstones of healthy intimacy.

The Missing Conversations

Growing up, boys are often taught the rules of competition but not connection. They learn how to win, how to toughen up, how to push forward—but rarely how to pause and check in with themselves or others.

For many men, this lack of guidance extends into adulthood. They're left to figure out boundaries and consent on their own, often through trial and error. Some develop a fear of being too assertive and withdraw completely, avoiding intimacy altogether. Others struggle with recognizing when they've overstepped, leading to guilt, confusion, or damaged relationships.

This gap in education isn't just personal—it's cultural. When we fail to teach men about consent and boundaries, we leave them unequipped to build the deep, respectful connections they crave.

Boundaries as Bridges

When Ryan expressed his discomfort with boundaries, I reassured him that he wasn't alone—and that our work together would be a safe space to explore and practice these skills.

One of the first things I emphasize with every client is that boundaries aren't barriers; they're bridges. They're not meant to separate us from others but to create a foundation of trust and mutual respect.

For men like Ryan, this can be a revelation. Boundaries aren't just something to respect in others—they're also something to set for themselves. When men learn to identify their own limits and communicate them clearly, they gain a deeper sense of agency and self-respect.

The Power of Consent

Consent, at its core, is about choice. It's about giving and receiving permission in a way that honors both parties. In my sessions, consent is woven into every interaction, from the moment a client walks through the door.

Before we begin, I always ask questions like:

"What feels comfortable for you today?"

"Is there anything you'd prefer we avoid?"

"How can I support you in feeling safe and at ease?"

These conversations aren't just practical—they're profoundly empowering. For many men, it's the first time they've been invited to pause and reflect on their own needs and comfort levels. It's also the first time they've experienced someone actively seeking their consent, without assumptions or pressure.

Lessons Beyond the Session

Ryan's journey with boundaries didn't end in my office—it extended into every area of his life. He began practicing what we discussed, both with himself and others.

One day, he shared a story with me about a friend who was going through a tough time. "Normally, I would've just jumped in with advice or tried to fix things," he said. "But this time, I asked him, 'Do you want me to listen, or would it help if I shared my thoughts?' And it completely changed the conversation. He actually thanked me for asking."

This might seem like a small shift, but for Ryan, it was transformative. By prioritizing consent and clarity, he was able to build a deeper, more respectful connection with someone he cared about.

A Culture of Respect

The lessons men learn about consent and boundaries in professional intimacy services go far beyond the personal—they ripple out into the culture around us. When men practice these skills, they're helping to create a world rooted in respect and care. They're showing that vulnerability is not a sign of weakness, that asking for what you need is an act of courage, and that listening can be just as powerful—if not more so—than leading.

In my sessions, I see men rediscover the beauty of mutual exchange. They learn that intimacy isn't about taking or controlling—it's about giving and receiving in harmony. They learn that "no" isn't rejection; it's clarity. And they learn that "yes" is most meaningful when it's freely given.

Ryan's Transformation

By the end of our time together, Ryan had a new perspective on what it meant to be close to others. "I used to think boundaries were about keeping people out," he said. "Now I see they're about making space for real connection."

This shift wasn't just theoretical—it was deeply felt. Ryan began rebuilding his relationships with more openness and honesty. He approached his friendships, his romantic life, and even his work with a renewed sense of respect and intention.

Why Boundaries Matter

Boundaries and consent aren't just abstract concepts—they're the foundation of healthy, fulfilling relationships. They allow us to show up authentically, to honor ourselves and others, and to build connections that are both safe and meaningful.

For men like Ryan, learning these skills can be life-changing. And for our culture as a whole, embracing these values can create a world where intimacy is no longer a source of fear or confusion, but one of joy, respect, and genuine connection.

Chapter 19: The Role of Platonic Intimacy in Healthy Relationships

When we think about intimacy, many of us naturally imagine romantic or sexual relationships. We tend to associate physical touch with desire, attraction, or love. But what if I told you that platonic intimacy—the kind of closeness shared between friends, family, and even acquaintances—can be just as powerful and important for building deep, trusting, and meaningful connections?

Platonic intimacy isn't about romantic love or sexual attraction. It's about cultivating a space of emotional vulnerability, trust, and connection that transcends the boundaries of traditional relationships. And surprisingly, one of the most effective ways to foster this type of intimacy is through touch—without it necessarily being sexual in nature.

In this chapter, I want to explore how platonic touch—whether it's a comforting hug, a friendly hand on the shoulder, or simply sitting close to someone you care about—can be an essential element of healthy relationships. I want to break down some misconceptions and share how touch, when used in a consensual and appropriate way, can deepen emotional bonds and enhance trust in every type of relationship.

Touch as a Foundation of Connection

Touch is often thought of as something that belongs only in intimate or romantic contexts, but in reality, it's a basic human need. Research has shown that touch can reduce stress, elevate mood, and promote feelings of security and belonging. It's not just romantic partners who benefit from these effects—everyone can.

Think about how you feel when a friend reaches out to pat you on the back after a difficult day, or how comforting it is when a family member hugs you without saying a word. These acts of touch—small but powerful—send a message of empathy and care. They remind us that we are not alone, that we are seen, and that we are loved in ways that go beyond words.

This is platonic intimacy in its purest form. It's the bond that exists between two people who care for each other, without any expectation of romance or sexual involvement. It's the trust that builds when you know someone has your back, and when physical touch is just one way of showing that.

Why Platonic Intimacy Matters

Platonic intimacy can be especially important for men, many of whom grow up with the message that touch is only appropriate within romantic or sexual relationships. Men are often conditioned to avoid being vulnerable with each other, to steer clear of physical affection, and to keep their emotional worlds hidden. This can create a sense of emotional isolation, even among close friends.

By allowing ourselves to be more open to non-sexual touch, we invite a sense of warmth and connection that is not only comforting but healing. Platonic touch helps men (and people in general) soften the emotional armor we sometimes build around ourselves to protect against vulnerability. It encourages emotional expression and nurtures bonds that are based on mutual respect and care.

What's more, platonic intimacy helps to cultivate a deeper sense of trust. Trust doesn't only come from verbal assurances; it is reinforced through shared experiences, actions, and yes—touch. When you trust someone enough to allow them to touch you in a non-sexual, caring way, it can make the relationship feel more grounded, more honest, and more deeply connected.

Examples of Platonic Intimacy in Action

You don't need to be in a romantic or sexual relationship to experience the benefits of touch. Here are some examples of platonic intimacy that you might already be familiar with or that you can begin to incorporate into your own relationships:

1. The Healing Hug

A hug from a close friend or family member can work wonders after a long, stressful day or when you're going through a tough time. There's something about the physical closeness and shared breath that can immediately make you feel understood and supported. It's a comforting form of touch that says, "I'm here for you," without needing any words.

2. The Friendly Touch

It can be as simple as a hand on the shoulder or a light touch on the arm when you're talking to someone. These subtle gestures communicate empathy and connection. In fact, they can have a calming effect, signaling to your nervous system that you're in a safe, supportive environment.

3. Cuddling with Friends or Family

This might sound surprising, but in some cultures, cuddling between friends or family members is completely natural. It doesn't have to be sexual or romantic—just sharing a close moment together on the couch while watching a movie or offering a snuggle after a rough day can deepen emotional closeness and help regulate your nervous system.

4. Group Activities that Encourage Physical Connection

Many group activities encourage non-sexual physical touch, like yoga, dance, or team sports. These activities foster a sense of community and connection through shared experience and mutual support. The touch that occurs during these activities isn't about sexuality; it's about being present with each other and creating a bond through the shared rhythm of movement.

5. The Casual Touch in Public

Sometimes it's as simple as a brief touch in public—a handshake, a pat on the back, or a friendly arm around the shoulder. These public displays of affection, within appropriate contexts, can normalize touch in friendships and remind people that their connection is valued.

How Platonic Intimacy Transforms Relationships

Incorporating more platonic touch into our relationships isn't just about creating moments of comfort; it also transforms the nature of the relationship itself. Let's take a closer look at how it impacts different kinds of relationships:

Friendships

In friendships, touch can be the glue that keeps the bond strong. A supportive touch during a conversation can communicate a level of understanding that words can't fully capture. It can help deepen the trust and emotional intimacy between friends, encouraging more open conversations about feelings, fears, and desires.

For men, who are often taught to hide their emotions, platonic touch can help create an emotional outlet. Friends who share physical affection—whether through hugs, pats, or friendly handshakes—are often able to communicate more openly and authentically with each other. This builds trust and a sense of safety that allows the relationship to flourish.

Family Relationships

Within family, platonic touch can reinforce the feeling of unconditional love. For example, a parent might give a hug or a kiss to show care and support for a child, even when the child is an adult. These acts of touch help reaffirm the family bond, offering a reminder that love and connection don't have to be verbalized all the time.

For older generations, touch can also be incredibly comforting. As parents or family members age, simple gestures like holding hands or offering a shoulder to lean on can communicate care and appreciation in ways that transcend words.

Professional Relationships

While touch in professional relationships is more limited, it's still possible to create a culture of platonic intimacy in the workplace. A handshake, a high-five after a successful project, or even a brief, supportive touch on the arm can create a sense of camaraderie and mutual respect among colleagues. Touch can contribute to team bonding and can reinforce a positive, supportive work environment.

The Power of Platonic Intimacy

When we allow touch to be a natural and integral part of all our relationships, not just the romantic ones, we begin to break down barriers that prevent us from fully connecting with others. Platonic intimacy—through comforting touches, friendly hugs, and shared moments of physical closeness—can create an environment of trust, empathy, and emotional safety.

By embracing platonic touch, we can build a world where emotional vulnerability is welcomed, and where physical connection is seen as a vital part of our well-being. This type of intimacy helps us feel seen, heard, and cared for—whether we are with friends, family, or coworkers.

Touch doesn't need to be sexual to be powerful. It's a fundamental way we communicate that we are human, that we are here for each other, and that we're not alone in this world. So, the next time you're with a close friend or family member, try adding a bit more touch to the equation—whether it's a heartfelt hug, a pat on the back, or simply sitting close together in shared silence. You might be surprised at how deeply it can transform your relationship.

Chapter 20: Dispelling the Shadows

When I first started offering professional intimacy services, I quickly realized that there were a lot of misconceptions about what my work actually involves. People would often express surprise, skepticism, or even discomfort when they found out what I do. It's understandable—this field is still relatively new, and society hasn't always been comfortable with the idea of professional touch and intimacy that isn't sexual in nature.

In this chapter, I want to address some of the myths surrounding professional intimacy services and break them down. The more we can demystify this work, the more we can open up space for people to embrace their needs for touch, emotional connection, and vulnerability, without shame.

Myth 1: All Professional Intimacy Services Are Sexual

This is perhaps the most common misconception. When people hear about cuddle therapy, intimacy coaching, or touch-based work, they immediately assume it's sexual. Let me be clear: professional intimacy work is not about sex. It's about touch, connection, and healing—none of which inherently have to be sexual.

Think about it: most of us, regardless of our sexual orientation or relationship status, need touch to thrive. We're social creatures, wired for connection. But in a world where physical affection is often commodified or sexualized, it can be challenging to separate intimacy from sexuality. That's where professional intimacy services come in—to provide nurturing, non-sexual touch in a safe, non-judgmental space.

I've had clients who came to me feeling nervous or even embarrassed, thinking that they were somehow "crossing a line." But once we establish clear, mutually agreed-upon boundaries, and they realize that this is a space where they can simply receive care and attention, their discomfort melts away. The touch is about restoring their sense of self-worth, feeling seen, and finding healing—not about sexual pleasure.

Myth 2: Professional Intimacy Services Are Only for People Who Are Lonely

Another misconception I frequently encounter is the idea that if someone is seeking professional intimacy services, it's because they're lonely or have no friends or relationships. While loneliness can be one reason someone might seek this kind of support, it's not the only one. People from all walks of life, with fulfilling relationships, use these services to enhance their well-being. Many of my clients are well-connected socially, have loving partners, or maintain strong family bonds.

They may be successful in their careers, active in their communities, and have an overall good life—but that doesn't mean they don't need touch and emotional connection. The modern world, with all its technological advancements, has ironically made it harder for people to experience authentic, meaningful touch. We're so often busy or distracted that we forget how deeply our bodies crave it. In many ways, seeking professional intimacy services is a way to reconnect with ourselves and others in a deeply human way.

Touch isn't just for lonely people—it's for anyone who recognizes that they have emotional needs that aren't being fully met, whether through friends, family, or romantic relationships. Many men, in particular, are conditioned to bottle up their emotions, and part of this work is helping them unlock their vulnerability in a safe, non-judgmental environment.

Myth 3: Only "Damaged" People Need Professional Intimacy Services

Another myth that persists is the belief that only people who are "damaged" or have deep emotional scars need to seek out professional intimacy services. Let's get one thing straight: everyone has emotional needs. Everyone could benefit from feeling cared for, nurtured, and seen.

Sometimes, the idea that only those who are "broken" or struggling with serious trauma or dysfunction need intimacy services can prevent people from seeking help. But the truth is, nurturing touch and emotional connection are human needs that should not be stigmatized. In fact, seeking out professional intimacy services can be a proactive way to nurture your emotional health and well-being, much in the same way that someone might go to therapy or engage in physical exercise.

Many of the men I work with are high-functioning, successful individuals who simply have unmet needs for touch and emotional support. They may not have suffered from abuse or trauma, but that doesn't mean they aren't experiencing loneliness or touch deprivation. The need for touch transcends whether someone has been "damaged"—it's a universal, natural aspect of being human.

Myth 4: Professional Intimacy Is Just an Excuse for Touching Strangers

Some people think that professional intimacy work is just a thinly veiled excuse for people to touch strangers inappropriately. This misconception comes from a misunderstanding of consent and boundaries.

In my sessions, boundaries are not only respected—they are the foundation of the work. Every session begins with a discussion about what is and isn't comfortable for the client. What is clear and explicit in my practice is that there is no room for ambiguity when it comes to respect and consent. The boundaries are set by the client, and they are always in control of the experience.

Professional intimacy services are about creating a safe, consensual space for people to explore their emotional and physical needs. Touch is used to offer comfort, healing, and connection—never as an excuse to cross boundaries or create discomfort. It's about respect, trust, and mutual understanding.

Myth 5: Only People with Specific Problems Need This Service

Some people assume that the only people who would seek out professional intimacy services are those with specific problems, such as sexual dysfunction or relationship issues. While these challenges can be one reason someone might choose to explore this type of work, it's far from the only reason.

Many men come to me simply because they recognize that they want to be more connected with themselves and others. They may want to improve their ability to communicate emotionally, explore their vulnerability, or experience physical touch in a safe and respectful environment. It's not always about a deep, underlying problem—it can be about enhancing emotional and physical well-being.

As men, we are often socialized to think that needing or wanting emotional care is a weakness, or that seeking help is a sign of being broken. But this is a harmful narrative. Taking the step to embrace vulnerability, express emotional needs, and seek nurturing touch is an act of strength, not weakness. It's about being human and honoring our natural need for connection.

Myth 6: All Therapists Are the Same

Finally, there's the idea that all professional intimacy services or cuddle therapists are the same. In reality, every practitioner has their own unique approach, experience, and background. What sets my work apart is the personalized, intentional, and compassionate nature of the services I provide. I take great care to create a space where my clients feel heard, understood, and respected.

My focus isn't simply on providing a hug or physical comfort, it's about creating a holistic experience that nurtures both the body and mind. I integrate my background in intimacy coaching and therapeutic touch to offer a transformative experience for men looking to heal and reconnect with themselves.

Final Thoughts

Professional intimacy services aren't about breaking taboos or indulging in unhealthy behaviors. They are about restoring balance to a world that has grown increasingly disconnected. My work is rooted in respect, consent, and trust, and it's designed to help people—especially men—rediscover their inherent worth, cultivate emotional connection, and embrace the healing power of touch.

I hope this chapter has helped clear up some of the misconceptions that surround this field. Professional intimacy services aren't about fulfilling some hidden agenda; they're about offering a simple yet powerful solution to a common problem in our modern lives: the lack of genuine human connection. And that is something that no one should feel ashamed of seeking.

Chapter 21: Why Some Men Seek a Male Touch and Intimacy Coach

Over the years, I've often been asked why a man might choose to work with me—a male touch and intimacy coach—instead of a female practitioner. It's a question that gets to the heart of what I do and why this work matters so deeply. For many men, this choice isn't about exclusion or preference in the traditional sense. It's about something more profound: safety, understanding, and the chance to explore parts of themselves they might not feel comfortable addressing elsewhere.

Let me walk you through some of the reasons men come to me and why having another man as their guide can be transformative.

Breaking Down the Walls of Shame

For many men, society has taught us that vulnerability equals weakness. That narrative can make it incredibly difficult to ask for help, let alone open up about something as personal as intimacy, touch, or emotional needs. When a man comes to me, he often carries a lifetime of messages telling him that his emotions or desire for connection are things to suppress.

Working with another man can feel like stepping into a mirror. It challenges the unspoken rule that men must always be stoic and self-sufficient. In this space, they see someone who understands that struggle intimately—not just because I've heard it from others, but because I've lived it myself.

When a man sees that I'm not judging him, it can start to dissolve the shame he's carried. There's a sense of "If you, as another man, can hold space for this, maybe it's okay for me to feel it too."

A Shared Understanding of the Male Experience

There's something powerful about being understood without needing to explain every nuance. Men often tell me that working with a male coach feels like they don't have to over-explain themselves.

We've walked similar roads, even if our paths have been different. We know what it's like to navigate societal expectations of masculinity, to feel the pressure to perform, to succeed, to "man up." There's an unspoken understanding that allows us to cut through the layers of pretense and get to the heart of the matter.

For example, one client told me he'd never felt comfortable talking about his need for touch with a female therapist because he worried it might be misinterpreted or dismissed. With me, he could say, "I just want to feel held without it meaning anything more than that."

And he knew I'd get it.

Reclaiming Connection Without Sexualization

Another reason some men seek out a male touch and intimacy coach is the opportunity to explore touch in a way that's non-sexual yet deeply affirming. For many men, touch has been tied almost exclusively to sexual contexts. They've never had the chance to experience nurturing, platonic touch without feeling conflicted or uncertain.

In a session with me, they can rediscover what it feels like to be touched with care and intention, free from any expectations. This is especially important for men who may have grown up in environments where physical affection was rare or absent.

For some, working with a female practitioner might feel fraught with layers of complexity—worry about being misunderstood, fear of appearing "needy," or even cultural conditioning that makes them hesitant to be vulnerable in front of a woman. With another man, those layers can fall away.

Challenging Internalized Homophobia or Bias

Interestingly, some men come to me specifically because they want to confront their own discomfort with male closeness. They may have grown up in environments where any kind of male intimacy was stigmatized or ridiculed. Working with me becomes an act of courage—a way to challenge those old beliefs and rewrite their narrative.

On Being Seen

One client shared that he'd avoided male friendships for most of his life because he was afraid of being perceived as gay, weak or "too soft." Our sessions became a safe space for him to explore what healthy male connection could look like. Over time, he began to embrace the idea that closeness with other men didn't diminish his masculinity—it enriched it.

Representation Matters

For gay, bisexual, or queer men, working with a male coach can feel especially affirming. It's an opportunity to explore their needs and desires in a space where they don't have to worry about judgment or misunderstanding.

One man told me he'd never felt fully seen by female practitioners because they didn't share his lived experience. With me, he could talk openly about his journey—his fears, his hopes, and his desire to feel connected to other men in ways that were both platonic and intimate.

The Power to Be Seen

At its core, choosing to work with a male touch and intimacy coach is about the power to be seen. To be seen as a whole person, not just through the lens of what society expects a man to be. It's about reclaiming the parts of yourself that have been hidden, denied, or neglected.

In our sessions, men often discover that their vulnerability is not a weakness but a strength. They learn that their need for touch, connection, and emotional expression is not something to be ashamed of—it's part of what makes them human.

So, why do men choose a male coach? Because sometimes, it takes another man to hold up the mirror and say, "You're okay just as you are. You're enough. And you deserve to be cared for."

If that resonates with you, know that this space exists. It's here, waiting, whenever you're ready to step into it.

Part 4: A New Vision for Male Connection

"The most basic of all human needs is the need to understand and be understood. The best way to understand people is to listen to them."

— Ralph G. Nichols

Chapter 22: What I've Learned About Men

When I first started this journey, I thought I had a decent understanding of men. I'd read the books, listened to the experts, and had my own personal experiences to draw from. But nothing could have prepared me for the profound lessons I'd learn through the work I do every day. Each session has been like a window into a hidden world—one that's often misunderstood, oversimplified, or outright ignored.

Men, as I've come to see them, are as complex and multifaceted as anyone else. Yet they face a unique set of challenges when it comes to expressing their needs, particularly when those needs revolve around touch and intimacy. This work has deepened my empathy, broadened my perspective, and taught me more about the human condition than I ever thought possible.

The Quiet Strength of Vulnerability

One of the most striking things I've learned is how resilient men are. Many of the men who walk through my door have carried immense emotional weight for years, sometimes decades. Whether it's unprocessed grief, the pain of rejection, or the lingering echoes of trauma, they've found ways to keep moving forward despite it all.

But resilience doesn't mean the absence of vulnerability. In fact, I've learned that true resilience often requires vulnerability—the willingness to confront what's uncomfortable, to open up even when it feels risky. For many men, this is uncharted territory. Society has told them for so long that vulnerability equals weakness, that to express emotion is to invite judgment or ridicule.

Yet in my sessions, I've witnessed something extraordinary: when given a safe space, men lean into their vulnerability with incredible courage. They tell me things they've never told anyone else. They cry despite the shame. They allow themselves to feel—not just in their minds, but in their bodies.

The Power of Touch

Touch has an extraordinary ability to bypass the walls men often build around their emotions. Words can be tricky —they require conscious thought, careful selection, and often carry the weight of past misunderstandings. But touch? Touch is immediate. It's primal. It speaks to parts of us that language can't reach.

I remember one client, David, who struggled to articulate how he was feeling. He'd been through a painful divorce and had spent years focusing on his career, avoiding any kind of emotional reflection. During our first session, he told me, "I don't know how to explain it. I just feel... numb."

As we began our session, I could see the tension in his body—his shoulders hunched, his hands clenched, his breathing shallow. But as the session progressed, something shifted. His muscles softened, his breathing slowed, and tears began to stream down his face. "I didn't even know I needed this," he whispered.

That's the power of touch. It allows men like David to access emotions they might not even realize they're holding onto. It gives them permission to feel without judgment, to let go without explanation.

Breaking the Myths

One of the biggest myths I've encountered is that men don't crave connection as deeply as women do. Nothing could be further from the truth. Men want to be seen, heard, and valued just as much as anyone else. They want to be held—not just physically, but emotionally and spiritually.

What often holds them back isn't a lack of desire but a lack of permission. From an early age, many men are taught to prioritize independence over interdependence, to hide their emotions rather than share them. They're given tools to compete but not to connect.

What I've learned is that when you strip away the societal expectations, the "rules" about what it means to be a man, what's left is a deep longing for connection. And when men are given the tools and the space to fulfill that longing, they thrive.

The Humanity of Men

The men I've worked with have taught me so much about humanity. They've reminded me that beneath the surface, we all want the same things: to be loved, to feel safe, to know we matter.

I've worked with men from all walks of life—CEOs, artists, teachers, fathers, sons. Each of them has brought their own unique story, but there's a common thread that connects them all: the desire to feel whole.

I think about Mark, a widowed father who spent so much of his life caring for others that he forgot how to care for himself. Or Alex, a young man navigating the loneliness of modern dating and the pressure to project a perfect life on social media. These men, and so many others, have shown me the beauty of human resilience and the transformative power of compassion.

The Lessons They've Taught Me

Through this work, I've learned to listen more deeply—not just to words, but to what lies beneath them. I've learned that silence can speak volumes, that a single tear can hold a lifetime of emotion, and that healing often happens in the spaces where words fail.

I've also learned that men are capable of immense growth. When given the tools and the support, they can unlearn the harmful narratives they've been taught and build lives that are more authentic, connected, and fulfilling.

Why This Work Matters

Every time I see a man leave a session standing a little taller, breathing a little easier, or smiling with a newfound sense of peace, I'm reminded why this work matters. It's not just about touch—it's about creating a space where men can rediscover themselves, where they can feel seen and valued without judgment.

The men I've worked with have taught me that vulnerability is a strength, that connection is a universal need, and that healing is always possible, no matter how long it's been. And for that, I am endlessly grateful.

If there's one thing I hope readers take away from this chapter, it's this: Men are not the unfeeling, stoic figures society often makes them out to be. They are human—beautifully, imperfectly human. And when we create spaces for them to be fully themselves, we all benefit.

Chapter 23: Changing the Narrative

For as long as I can remember, society has painted a narrow picture of what it means to be a man. Men are strong, stoic, and self-reliant—or so the story goes. They don't cry, they don't ask for help, and they certainly don't admit to feeling lonely or needing affection.

This narrative has been so deeply ingrained in our culture that many men don't even realize they're living by its rules. They might know they feel disconnected, frustrated, or hollow, but they can't always pinpoint why. And when they do, shame often stops them from saying it out loud.

The truth is, this story we've been telling about men isn't just outdated—it's harmful. It creates barriers to connection, isolates men from their own emotions, and reinforces the toxic idea that needing care is a sign of weakness.

It's time to change that narrative.

Why the Old Narrative No Longer Works

The world is changing, and with it, so are the roles and expectations of men. We're starting to see more open conversations about mental health, emotional intelligence, and vulnerability. But there's still a long way to go, particularly when it comes to how we view men and their emotional needs.

The old narrative—the one that says men are supposed to be "tough" and "unbreakable"—doesn't leave much room for humanity. It ignores the fact that men, like everyone else, are wired for connection. Humans are social creatures, and touch, affection, and emotional intimacy aren't luxuries; they're necessities.

When we tell boys and men they should suppress those needs, we set them up for a lifetime of emotional isolation. We see the consequences in rising rates of depression, anxiety, and loneliness among men. We see it in strained relationships, in unhealthy coping mechanisms, and in the heartbreaking statistic that men are far more likely than women to die by suicide.

This isn't just a personal issue—it's a societal one. And it's one we can't afford to ignore any longer.

Destigmatizing Touch

One of the most powerful ways we can start shifting the narrative is by addressing the stigma around touch. For many men, touch is something that's either sexualized or absent. There's very little room in between.

Platonic touch—whether it's a hug, a pat on the back, or a hand on the shoulder—is something many men are starved of. It's not because they don't want it, but because they've been conditioned to see it as unmanly or inappropriate.

I've had clients tell me they can't remember the last time they were hugged, or that the only touch they experience is transactional—like a handshake—or confined to romantic or sexual contexts. This deprivation isn't just sad; it's harmful.

Touch is a basic human need. It reduces stress, lowers blood pressure, and releases oxytocin, the "bonding hormone." It helps us feel seen and valued, reminds us we're not alone, and fosters a sense of safety and belonging.

When men are denied access to touch, they're denied access to one of the most fundamental ways we connect as humans.

Rethinking Masculinity

If we're going to change the narrative, we need to rethink what it means to be a man. Masculinity doesn't have to mean emotional stoicism or physical toughness. It can mean compassion, vulnerability, and the courage to express what you need.

I've worked with men who were initially hesitant to try professional intimacy services because they felt it went against the image of masculinity they'd been taught. But after experiencing the power of touch and connection, many of them described feeling more "manly" than ever—not because they were performing some cultural ideal, but because they were embracing their full humanity.

It's not about throwing out masculinity altogether; it's about expanding it. Men can be strong and vulnerable, independent and deeply connected. *These things aren't mutually exclusive.*

How Society Can Foster Healthier Connections

Changing the narrative isn't just about individual men—it's about society as a whole. We all have a role to play in fostering healthier forms of male connection.

Start Young
Boys should be taught from an early age that it's okay to express their feelings, to ask for help, and to value connection. This means creating environments—at home, in schools, and in communities—where emotional expression is encouraged, not ridiculed.

Lead by Example
Men who are in positions of influence—whether as fathers, mentors, or public figures—have a unique opportunity to model vulnerability and healthy connection. When men see others embracing these qualities, it gives them permission to do the same.

Normalize Touch
We need to normalize platonic touch between men. This could be as simple as encouraging a culture of hugging among friends or creating more opportunities for non-sexual physical connection in therapeutic or communal settings.

Challenge Stigma
Whether it's through media representation, public discourse, or personal conversations, we need to challenge the stigma around men seeking help, whether for mental health, professional intimacy, or other forms of support.

Create Safe Spaces
Safe spaces—like the sessions I offer—are crucial for helping men explore their needs without fear of judgment. But these spaces shouldn't be confined to therapy rooms. They can exist in friendships, workplaces, and communities too.

A Story of Transformation

I'll never forget the story of one client, James, a father in his late 40s who came to me feeling completely burned out.

He was the rock for his family, his workplace, and his friends, but he had no one to lean on himself.

In our sessions, James began to unpack the narrative he'd been living: that he needed to be the "strong one" all the time, that asking for help was a sign of failure. Over time, as he allowed himself to experience touch and connection, something shifted.

"I didn't recognize the absence until I felt the presence," he told me one day. "It's like I've been carrying a weight I didn't even know was there."

James's story is one of many, but it speaks to the heart of why this work is so important. When we create spaces for men to reconnect with themselves and others, we help them reclaim parts of their humanity that might have been buried for years.

Why This Matters

Changing the narrative isn't just about helping men—it's about creating a more compassionate, connected society for everyone. When men are allowed to express their emotions, seek connection, and embrace vulnerability, they become better partners, fathers, friends, and leaders.

This isn't about fixing men; it's about freeing them. Freeing them from the outdated stories they've been told about what it means to be a man. Freeing them to feel, to connect, and to thrive.

If there's one thing I've learned from this work, it's that change is possible. It starts with small steps—like a hug, a conversation, or a moment of shared vulnerability. And over time, those small steps add up to something extraordinary: a new narrative, one where men are seen, valued, and embraced for all that they are.

Chapter 24: A Vision for a New Masculinity

As we approach the end of this journey, I want to offer a vision—one that transcends the old ideas of masculinity that have shaped so many of us. It's a vision of a new masculinity that embraces emotional expression, vulnerability, and physical connection without shame. It's a vision where men are no longer forced to bottle up their feelings, hide their need for touch, or feel like they have to constantly perform a version of strength that leaves no room for the fullness of their humanity.

This new masculinity doesn't just honor men's emotional and physical needs—it celebrates them. It doesn't shame men for feeling deeply, for needing affection, or for seeking connection. Instead, it empowers men to express themselves freely, to embrace vulnerability as a source of strength, and to connect with others in ways that are nurturing and supportive.

For far too long, society has placed men in a narrow box—one that demands stoicism, emotional restraint, and a disconnection from anything that might be perceived as "soft" or "weak." But I believe it's time to break free from these outdated norms. The world needs a new definition of masculinity—one that recognizes that true strength comes from embracing all parts of ourselves, including the emotional and physical needs that are often overlooked or dismissed.

Redefining Strength

In the traditional model of masculinity, strength is often measured by physical power, dominance, and the ability to endure hardship without showing any signs of weakness. Men are taught to hold their emotions in check, to hide their tears, and to act as if they don't need anyone. But real strength, I believe, lies in the ability to be vulnerable, to express emotions authentically, and to seek help when you need it.

It takes immense strength to admit that you need support, that you long for connection, or that you're hurting. True strength is in being honest with yourself and others, in allowing yourself to be seen in all your complexity—flaws, fears, desires, and all. The bravest thing you can do is to embrace your emotions and let others see the real you, not the version of yourself you think you're supposed to be.

The Power of Emotional Expression

One of the core elements of this new masculinity is emotional expression. For too long, men have been told that expressing emotions is a sign of weakness. We've been told to push through pain, and to never let our guard down. This has led to countless men suffering in silence, feeling isolated, misunderstood, and disconnected from their own emotions.

But emotional expression is vital for mental and emotional well-being. It allows us to process our feelings, to heal from trauma, and to connect more deeply with others. Men need spaces where they can feel safe to express their emotions without fear of judgment or ridicule. This means giving yourself permission to cry, to talk about your fears, to admit when you're struggling. It means not having to pretend you have it all together all the time.

Expressing emotions doesn't make you less of a man—it makes you a more complete one. It allows you to build deeper, more meaningful relationships and to show up in your life as your authentic self.

Embracing the Need for Touch

Another crucial aspect of this new masculinity is the acknowledgment of touch as a natural, essential need. For many men, touch has been relegated to sexual contexts or dismissed as something unnecessary or inappropriate. Men are often taught to be independent, to tough it out, and to avoid physical contact unless it's with a romantic partner or in moments of crisis.

But the truth is that touch is a basic human need that affects our well-being on every level. Whether it's a hug from a friend, a hand on your shoulder in support, or a moment of quiet physical connection with a loved one, touch helps us feel grounded, connected, and cared for. It is deeply nurturing and healing. Touch reduces stress, boosts mood, fosters trust, and helps us feel less alone in the world.

This new masculinity embraces the idea that touch is essential for men's emotional health. It encourages men to seek out and offer touch in a way that is respectful, consensual, and supportive. Touching friends, family, or even a therapist doesn't make you less of a man—it makes you human. It connects you to others, builds empathy, and helps you process your emotions.

A Call to Action: Embrace Your Full Humanity

As I write these words, I'm thinking of all the men I've worked with—each one coming to me with their own struggles, their own stories, and their own desires for connection. What strikes me most is how many of them have been so starved for the simple things: touch, attention, presence, and space to be vulnerable. Many of them have been taught to repress their needs, to hide their true selves, and to fit into a mold of masculinity that no longer serves them.

I want to invite you, as a man reading this, to step into the fullness of who you are. It's time to embrace your emotional depth, to express your feelings without shame, and to seek the touch and connection that you deserve. It's time to break free from the belief that you have to do it all alone, that you have to be "strong" at the cost of your own well-being.

The world needs you to be more than just the strong, silent type. The world needs you to be fully present—emotionally, physically, and spiritually. It needs you to show up as your authentic self, with all the depth, vulnerability, and humanity that makes you who you are. You don't have to fit into anyone's narrow definition of masculinity. You get to define what it means to be a man on your own terms.

Building a Supportive Community

One of the first steps toward creating this new masculinity is surrounding yourself with a supportive community. You don't have to go through this alone. Seek out spaces where you can express yourself openly, where vulnerability is encouraged, and where touch is welcomed in a healthy and consensual way. This might be with close friends, family, or through professional intimacy services that provide a safe environment for connection.

There are many ways to build a community that nurtures your emotional and physical needs. Whether it's joining a men's group, practicing yoga, or participating in activities that encourage non-sexual touch (like dance or group meditation), you can create an environment where emotional expression and touch are not only accepted but celebrated. You don't have to hide who you are or suppress your need for connection.

The Road Ahead

As we move forward into this new era of masculinity, I encourage you to take small steps toward embracing this new way of being. Start by being honest with yourself about your needs—emotionally, physically, and relationally. Acknowledge the areas where you've been holding back, where you've been afraid to show vulnerability or seek connection.

Remember, this journey isn't about perfection. It's about progress. It's about creating a space where you can be yourself, unapologetically, and where you can embrace the full spectrum of your humanity. The world needs men who are willing to be vulnerable, who are unafraid of expressing their emotions, and who understand that true strength comes from connecting deeply with themselves and others.

Together, we can reshape what it means to be a man in this world. We can create a new narrative—one that values emotional intelligence, nurtures connection, and embraces touch as a source of healing and growth. It's time for a new masculinity. It's time to live authentically, without shame, and to build the world of connection we all deserve.

The journey starts with you.

Chapter 25: Building a Touch-Supportive Community

The importance of touch for emotional well-being can't be overstated. However, in a society where many men are conditioned to suppress their emotional needs, finding ways to receive and give healthy, consensual touch can feel challenging. But what if you could build a supportive community where platonic touch is embraced? A space where physical connection isn't laden with judgment, shame, or expectations, but rather celebrated as a natural, healing, and human need?

In this chapter, I'll walk you through the steps of creating a touch-supportive community—whether it's through friendship circles, group activities, or even exploring touch-based therapy. The goal is to empower you to embrace your need for connection in a healthy, nurturing, and non-judgmental way.

Why Touch-Supportive Communities Matter

When I first began offering professional intimacy services, many of my clients came to me with the understanding that they were missing something fundamental in their lives: genuine, non-sexual touch. What they often didn't realize was how rare and precious these types of experiences are for men. Society places so many restrictions on men's emotional expression, and this translates into their physical lives too. We are taught that touch is something reserved for romantic or sexual relationships, not as a tool for healing, comfort, or emotional connection between friends or community members.

But touch is inherently social. It's part of what makes us human. From a pat on the back to a handshake to a comforting hug, physical touch is a fundamental way we express care, empathy, and support. Unfortunately, many men grow up learning to suppress this need, fearing vulnerability or feeling shame about it. Building a touch-supportive community is about breaking down those barriers, learning to give and receive touch freely, and creating a safe space where men can feel supported, connected, and understood.

Step 1: Create Safe, Supportive Friendships

The foundation of any touch-supportive community is healthy, supportive friendships. Men often feel isolated when it comes to expressing emotional vulnerability, particularly with physical touch. But one of the first places to start is by normalizing these needs within your existing friendships.

A simple way to create this space is by opening up about your need for platonic touch. Vulnerability breeds vulnerability—when one person shares their need for connection, it often invites others to do the same. It might be a conversation that starts with, "Hey, I've been thinking a lot about the importance of touch in my life, and I want to create more opportunities for healthy, non-sexual touch. Would you be open to giving me a hug, or maybe we could just sit together?"

Start small. Maybe you all gather for a movie night and, at the end of the evening, share a group hug or just sit together on the couch, allowing the energy to be comforting and present. As you build this trust and comfort with your friends, it will naturally become easier to lean into touch, whether it's a friendly hand on the shoulder, a comforting embrace during a difficult time, or just a casual high-five or fist bump.

Step 2: Seek Out Platonic Touch Experiences

If you feel like you're struggling to find touch-supportive environments within your current circles, there are plenty of other ways to create those opportunities. The beauty of touch-based activities is that they can serve as a bridge to connecting with people in a consensual, safe, and non-sexual way. Below are some suggestions for activities that can encourage touch in a supportive, respectful, and nurturing manner:

Yoga

Yoga is an excellent place to begin cultivating a supportive touch community. Many yoga practices emphasize mindful touch—whether through gentle adjustments by instructors or group activities that involve partner poses. It's a way to connect with others while also tuning into your own body and emotional needs. In certain styles of yoga, like partner yoga, you're invited to work with others in a way that emphasizes trust, communication, and physical support. It's a great opportunity to embrace touch as a way of supporting one another's journey.

Group Meditation or Breathwork Circles

Meditation and breathwork aren't typically thought of as "touch-based" activities, but they can be powerful vehicles for connection. In group settings, you can often find yourself sitting or lying in proximity to others, which provides a sense of connection without needing to directly touch. That shared space can bring a sense of closeness, and many groups will encourage gentle touch in the form of hand-holding or placing a hand on a friend's shoulder to create a deeper sense of grounding. These spaces can encourage emotional release and foster the type of vulnerability where touch can be used as a healing tool.

Dance and Movement Groups

Dance can be another great avenue for touch. Whether it's a social dance class like salsa, swing, or ballroom, or even more somatic practices like ecstatic dance, there's an inherent amount of touch and connection that happens in these spaces. Dance allows you to interact with others, respecting boundaries, while creating physical closeness through coordinated movement. What's great about these environments is that the focus is on the shared experience of movement, which often encourages connection and touch without feeling awkward or forced.

In these spaces, men can explore how their bodies interact with others in a consensual way, learn how to express emotions through movement, and practice connecting without the pressure of expectations.

Step 3: Explore Professional Intimacy Services

If building touch-supportive communities within your friendships or activities doesn't quite meet your emotional needs, professional intimacy services are another option. These services offer a safe, structured environment where you can receive non-sexual touch while exploring your emotions, vulnerability, and connection with others.

As I've discussed in earlier chapters, professional intimacy services are not about fulfilling romantic or sexual needs but about healing and nurturing the human need for touch. Whether through cuddle therapy, bodywork, or other forms of professional support, these services can provide a much-needed space for you to experience the benefits of healthy touch in a safe and therapeutic environment.

Step 4: Communicate Boundaries and Consent

In any touch-supportive community, clear communication is key. This means being open about your own needs, and listening to others' boundaries with respect. When it comes to touch, we all have different comfort levels and experiences, so it's essential to establish consent. Be mindful that the most important aspect of building a touch-supportive community is that everyone involved feels safe, respected, and understood.

Before any physical connection occurs, have open discussions with your friends, family, or group members about comfort levels, what touch feels good, and what might be off-limits. Consent is not just about saying "yes" or "no" —it's about continuously checking in with each other, making sure that everyone's needs are being met, and creating a space where emotional and physical boundaries are respected.

Fostering Connection Through Touch

Building a touch-supportive community isn't just about finding people who are open to touch—it's about creating a safe space where emotional vulnerability, empathy, and respect for boundaries come first. Touch can be a powerful tool for connection, healing, and emotional growth. As men, we have an incredible opportunity to redefine what it means to connect with each other beyond the traditional confines of sexuality. By cultivating spaces where we can embrace touch in all its forms—whether through friendship, group activities, or professional services—we can begin to break down the walls that keep us isolated and disconnected.

Creating a touch-supportive community is an act of self-care, and it can help foster the deep connections we all crave. It's time to embrace our need for healthy touch and explore the ways we can share that need with others in a way that feels nourishing and genuine. Touch is not just for intimate partners—it's for friends, for community, and for ourselves. The first step is to start the conversation.

On Being Seen

Chapter 26: A Guide to Healthy Touch

Touch is one of the most fundamental ways we connect with others and ourselves. From the moment we're born, touch is a form of communication, comfort, and connection. However, in adulthood, many men find themselves disconnected from this powerful tool—either because they've been conditioned to suppress their emotional needs or because they've never been taught how to use touch in healthy, non-sexual ways. In this chapter, I'll explore different types of touch and how they can be used to promote well-being. I'll also share how you can incorporate healthy touch into your own life to feel more connected, grounded, and emotionally supported.

The Power of Touch

Touch has incredible power. It can calm us, soothe our anxieties, boost our mood, and make us feel connected. As men, we might sometimes feel conflicted about our need for touch, especially when it's not part of a romantic or sexual context. But here's the truth: touch is a basic human need, and it's a healthy part of expressing care, love, and friendship. Just because you're not in a romantic relationship doesn't mean you can't experience the benefits of non-sexual, platonic touch.

Whether it's comforting yourself through self-touch, sharing a hug with a close friend, or simply sitting side by side with someone in quiet presence, there are many ways to experience the profound benefits of human connection through touch.

1. Comforting Touch: The Healing Hug

One of the most universally understood forms of touch is comforting touch—usually associated with a hug, a gentle touch on the shoulder, or a hand placed on someone's arm. Comforting touch is about offering emotional reassurance and safety. It's the touch you might give a friend or family member when they're going through a difficult time, or the kind of embrace you share after a long separation.

Benefits of comforting touch:

• **Reduces stress:** Physical contact like hugging or a gentle touch has been shown to reduce cortisol (the stress hormone) and release oxytocin, the bonding hormone that promotes feelings of happiness and trust.

• **Calms anxiety:** When we're anxious or overwhelmed, comforting touch can bring a sense of calm. It signals to our nervous system that we are safe and not alone.

• **Fosters connection:** Comforting touch helps strengthen bonds between people. It shows care, empathy, and understanding.

How to practice comforting touch:

• Hug a friend or family member when they're feeling down or stressed.

• Place a hand on someone's shoulder or back when they're upset.

• Give yourself a hug—wrap your arms around yourself and hold tight for a few moments. This simple practice can help soothe anxiety and provide comfort when you need it most.

2. Nurturing Touch: Self-Care and Healing

Nurturing touch is about self-care and healing. It's the kind of touch we often forget to give ourselves—simple acts of tenderness that help us slow down, relax, and reconnect with our bodies. Nurturing touch can come in many forms, from rubbing your own shoulders to giving yourself a gentle foot massage after a long day.

Benefits of nurturing touch:

• **Relieves tension:** Self-massage or gentle touch helps release physical tension that accumulates throughout the day.

• **Improves body awareness:** Taking the time to care for your body with nurturing touch helps you become more attuned to your physical needs.

• **Boosts mood:** Self-touch, like running your hands through your hair or rubbing your temples, can be soothing and uplifting, helping to combat feelings of fatigue or stress.

How to practice nurturing touch:

• Try giving yourself a hand massage. Start by massaging your palms, then move to your fingers and wrists. Pay attention to the sensations you feel as you touch yourself.

- Take a few moments each day to rub your own shoulders, especially if you feel tense. This can be a quick but effective way to release tightness.

- Consider a nightly routine of massaging your feet. This can help ground you, especially after a long or stressful day.

3. Platonic Touch: Bonding and Connection

Platonic touch is the touch we share with friends, family, or even acquaintances that isn't sexual or romantic in nature. It can be as simple as a pat on the back, holding hands with a friend, or linking arms with someone in a gesture of camaraderie. Platonic touch fosters a sense of closeness, trust, and affection between people.

Benefits of platonic touch:

- **Strengthens friendships**: Small, non-sexual touches like a handshake or a brief hug can help reinforce the bond between friends and create a sense of belonging.

- **Promotes trust:** When you touch someone respectfully and without expectation, it builds trust and mutual understanding.

- **Reduces loneliness:** In a world where many men feel isolated, platonic touch can help bridge the gap and offer a sense of connection and community.

How to practice platonic touch:

- Offer a hug when greeting a friend or saying goodbye.

- Give a brief touch on the arm when showing appreciation or encouragement.

- Hold hands with a friend in a moment of connection. This can be especially meaningful when walking together or during shared moments of joy or support.

4. Protective Touch: Offering Care and Reassurance

Protective touch is a form of touch that conveys care and the desire to keep someone safe. This could be a hand on someone's back as you guide them through a crowd or the act of offering a comforting touch during a tense or uncertain situation. Protective touch can feel grounding, reassuring, and stabilizing.

Benefits of protective touch:

- Fosters safety: Protective touch sends the message that the person is being looked after and that they're not alone in challenging situations.

- Promotes feelings of trust: When we feel physically protected, we are more likely to open up emotionally and feel supported.

- Reduces feelings of vulnerability: Touch can help mitigate feelings of fear or anxiety, especially in difficult circumstances.

How to practice protective touch:

- Gently guide a friend or loved one with a hand on their back or shoulder, offering physical reassurance.

- If someone is feeling nervous or fearful, place a hand on their arm or hold their hand, letting them know you're there for them.

- In moments of uncertainty, take a deep breath and place a reassuring touch on someone's hand or shoulder to offer comfort.

5. Reassuring Touch: A Simple Reminder of Presence

Reassuring touch is often understated but incredibly powerful. It's the simple gesture that says "I'm here for you" —a hand on the knee, a soft touch on the wrist, or a reassuring rub on the back. This type of touch is particularly useful during times of uncertainty or emotional vulnerability.

Benefits of reassuring touch:

- **Promotes emotional regulation:** Reassuring touch helps calm the nervous system, making it easier to navigate stressful or difficult situations.

- **Encourages presence:** It reminds us that someone is there, physically and emotionally, offering support without needing words.

- **Affirms connection:** Reassuring touch lets others know they are not alone in their experience.

How to practice reassuring touch:

- When a friend or loved one is going through a hard time, place a hand on their arm or leg as a simple but powerful reminder that you are there for them.

- Use gentle, comforting touch in conversation to convey empathy or understanding. A simple hand on the back or a shoulder squeeze can make all the difference.

Embracing Healthy Touch

Touch is an essential part of the human experience. It allows us to connect, heal, and grow. As men, we don't have to limit our understanding of touch to romantic or sexual contexts. Healthy touch can take many forms—comforting, nurturing, platonic, protective, and reassuring—and each form offers its own unique set of benefits. The key is learning to embrace touch as a natural, vital part of life and giving yourself permission to receive and share it in healthy, respectful ways.

Remember, touch is not about a transaction; it's about connection. Whether you're hugging a friend, massaging your own shoulders, or offering a comforting touch, each act of touch can create moments of healing, reassurance, and emotional growth. It's time to break free from the limitations of societal norms and embrace touch as the powerful tool for connection and well-being that it truly is. Start small, and allow yourself to experience the many ways touch can enrich your life.

A Call to Connection

As I reflect on the stories I've shared throughout this book, one thing becomes crystal clear: men's needs for touch, intimacy, and connection are not just valid—they are essential. Yet, too often, these needs are dismissed, misunderstood, or buried beneath layers of societal expectations.

If you're reading this and something inside you resonates, I want to reassure you: there's nothing wrong with you for craving connection. You're not "weak" or "needy." You're human. The desire for touch, affection, and emotional closeness isn't just natural—it's one of the most beautiful parts of being alive.

A Safe Place to Start

For many men, the hardest part of this journey is taking the first step. Maybe you've been taught to believe that vulnerability is a sign of failure, or that seeking help means you're broken. Maybe you're unsure of where to even begin.

Let me tell you this: It's okay to feel uncertain. It's okay to have questions, to feel hesitant, or even to doubt whether this is for you. What matters is that you're here, reading these words, and opening yourself to the possibility that there might be something more waiting for you—a life filled with deeper connection, self-acceptance, and fulfillment.

That's what this work is about. It's not just about touch—it's about what touch represents: safety, trust, care, and the reminder that you don't have to navigate life's challenges alone.

An Invitation

If you've felt moved by the stories in this book, I want to extend an invitation. Whether you're seeking healing, connection, or simply a safe space to be seen and valued, professional intimacy services like mine can provide a unique opportunity to explore those needs.

In my practice, every session is designed to honor your boundaries, meet you where you are, and create a space of mutual trust and respect. Together, we'll work to dissolve the emotional armoring that might be keeping you from experiencing the love and connection you deserve.

Whether it's through mindful touch, deep listening, or simply being present with another human being, these sessions aren't about "fixing" you. They're about helping you reconnect with the parts of yourself that have always been whole.

Starting Conversations in Your Own Life

Of course, this isn't just about professional services. You can start exploring connection in your daily life as well. Here are a few ways to take small but meaningful steps toward greater intimacy:

Reach Out: If there's someone in your life—a friend, partner, or family member—you trust, consider opening up a conversation about your feelings or needs. Sometimes, simply saying, "I've been thinking a lot about how important connection is to me," can be a powerful way to start.

Normalize Touch: If you feel comfortable, try incorporating more platonic touch into your relationships. Whether it's a hug, a pat on the back, or even sitting close to someone, these small gestures can foster a deeper sense of connection.

Educate Yourself: Books, podcasts, and resources about vulnerability, intimacy, and emotional well-being can provide valuable insights and encouragement. The more you understand yourself, the easier it becomes to share that understanding with others.

Seek Support: Whether it's a trusted therapist, coach, or practitioner, finding someone who can hold space for your journey can make all the difference.

Next Steps with Me

If you're ready to take that first step, I'd love to support you. Through my services—ranging from touch therapy to sacred intimacy sessions—we can work together to explore what connection means for you and how to integrate it into your life.

You can learn more about my services, including how to book a session, by visiting my website:

www.trevorjamesla.com for intimacy coaching, touch and cuddle therapy, massage and sacred intimacy.

If you'd like to have a conversation first, I also offer Clarity Calls. These calls provide an opportunity to ask questions, share your thoughts, and decide if this is the right path for you.

A Final Thought

Before we part ways, I want to leave you with this: Your needs are not a burden. Your desire for touch, intimacy, and connection is not something to be ashamed of. It's something to honor.

In a world that often tells men to tough it out, I hope this book has shown you that there's another way—a way that values your humanity, your vulnerability, and your capacity to give and receive love.

You deserve connection. You deserve care. And you deserve a life where your needs are not just acknowledged but celebrated.

So, here's my call to you: Take the next step, whatever that looks like for you. Whether it's reaching out to someone, starting a new conversation, or booking your first session, know that you don't have to do it alone.

You're not just allowed to seek connection—you're meant for it.

Epilogue

As I sit here reflecting on the journey this book has taken us on, I feel a profound sense of gratitude—for the men who have trusted me with their stories, for the power of connection that continues to transform lives, and for you, dear reader, for walking this path with me.

Throughout these pages, we've explored the many ways men navigate the world of touch, intimacy, and connection. We've delved into the barriers that society has placed around vulnerability and the quiet courage it takes to break them down. We've celebrated moments of transformation, where men have reclaimed parts of themselves they thought were lost or forbidden. And we've imagined a future where masculinity is not defined by suppression but by expression, where connection is not a luxury but a birthright.

What I hope you take away from this journey is a simple truth: we are all wired for connection. No matter how strong or independent we might appear, no matter the masks we wear or the walls we build, the need to be seen, to be held, to be known is universal. It is not a weakness. It is not something to be ashamed of. It is what makes us human.

I think often of the men I've worked with—their stories, their struggles, their triumphs. I think of the man who finally asked his partner for the touch he craved, the one who embraced his tears for the first time, the one who discovered that vulnerability didn't diminish his masculinity but expanded it. Each of them has taught me something about resilience, about courage, and about the profound beauty of being seen for who we truly are.

And now, as you close this book, I want to leave you with a question: What would it look like for you to embrace the power to be seen?

Maybe it's allowing yourself to ask for what you need, without apology. Maybe it's holding space for the men in your life to do the same. Maybe it's simply starting a conversation about touch, intimacy, or connection—topics that are often shrouded in silence but are so vital to our well-being.

The world needs more of this. It needs more men who are willing to show up as their full, authentic selves. It needs more people who are willing to listen without judgment, to hold space for vulnerability, and to celebrate the courage it takes to be human.

I don't pretend to have all the answers, but I do know this: the journey toward connection is worth it. It's not always easy, and it often requires us to step into uncomfortable places, but the rewards—the deeper relationships, the sense of wholeness, the quiet joy of being truly seen—are immeasurable.

So, as you move forward, I encourage you to carry this message with you. Let it inspire you to seek connection in your own life, to extend compassion to yourself and others, and to embrace the incredible power of touch, intimacy, and vulnerability.

Thank you for sharing this journey with me. I hope it has sparked something within you—a curiosity, a question, a new way of seeing yourself or the world. And I hope, above all, that it reminds you of the beauty and strength that come from allowing yourself to be fully, unapologetically seen.

Here's to connection, to courage, and to the power of being human!

Extras

Resources for Further Exploration

If this book has sparked your curiosity about touch, intimacy, and connection, you might want to dive deeper. Below is a list of resources to help you on your journey—books, support groups, and organizations dedicated to fostering healthy relationships and emotional well-being, specifically for men.

Note: *The resources, books, support groups, and organizations mentioned in this book are provided for informational purposes only. They are not intended to serve as endorsements or guarantees of effectiveness. While I have made every effort to recommend reputable and helpful resources, I encourage readers to exercise their own judgment and discretion when seeking support or using these materials.*

Recommended Readings

Books on Masculinity and Emotional Health

Daring Greatly by Brené Brown – A profound exploration of vulnerability and why it's the key to meaningful relationships.

The Mask of Masculinity by Lewis Howes – A guide to breaking down societal pressures and living authentically.

Hold Me Tight by Dr. Sue Johnson – A powerful resource for understanding emotional connection in relationships.

Books on Touch and Intimacy

Touch: The Science of Hand, Heart, and Mind by David J. Linden – A fascinating look at the role touch plays in human connection.

The Art of Receiving and Giving: The Wheel of Consent by Betty Martin – Essential reading for understanding boundaries, consent, and shared touch.

Books on Emotional Intelligence

Emotional Intelligence 2.0 by Travis Bradberry and Jean Greaves – A practical guide to understanding and improving your emotional awareness.

Support Groups and Organizations

Men's Support Networks

The Mankind Project – A global network offering men's groups, retreats, and resources to help men grow emotionally and spiritually.

Good Men Project – A community dedicated to fostering conversations about masculinity and connection.

Touch and Intimacy Resources

Cuddle Sanctuary – A resource hub for platonic touch workshops and professional cuddle therapy.

Wheel of Consent by Betty Martin – Offers free tools and resources to explore boundaries and consent.

Mental Health Support

HeadsUpGuys – A men's mental health resource specializing in depression and emotional resilience.

BetterHelp – Online counseling with licensed therapists, including those specializing in men's emotional health.

FAQ: Common Questions About Professional Intimacy Services

Seeking professional intimacy services can feel like a big step, and it's natural to have questions or concerns. Here are some of the most common ones I hear:

1. Isn't it embarrassing to pay for intimacy or touch?
Not at all. In fact, seeking professional intimacy services shows self-awareness and a commitment to your well-being. Think of it as hiring a personal trainer for your emotional and physical health.

2. Will people judge me if they find out I use these services?
While societal stigma exists, choosing to prioritize your needs is a brave and healthy decision. Many clients find it empowering to share their experiences, helping others see these services in a new light.

3. Is it weird to crave touch if I'm not in a relationship?
Absolutely not. Humans are wired to need touch, regardless of their relationship status. Craving connection is a natural part of being human, not a reflection of inadequacy.

4. Are these sessions sexual?
No, professional intimacy services like mine focus on creating safe, nurturing spaces for non-sexual touch and connection. Consent and clear boundaries are at the heart of every session.

5. What if I feel nervous or awkward during my first session?

It's completely normal to feel nervous. Many clients are unsure of what to expect at first. My job is to help you feel at ease by guiding you through the process and creating a space where you feel safe to relax and be yourself.

6. Do I need to talk about my emotions during a session?

Only if you want to. Some clients enjoy sharing their thoughts and feelings, while others prefer to experience the session quietly. There's no right or wrong way—this is your time, and it's all about what feels best for you.

7. How do I know if this is right for me?

If you've ever felt isolated, touch-deprived, or disconnected, professional intimacy services might be worth exploring. You can start with a Clarity Call to discuss your needs and get a better sense of whether this work is the right fit for you.

8. Are there any rules or expectations I should know about?

Yes. Each session begins with a clear discussion of boundaries and mutual expectations. Respect, consent, and open communication are essential, ensuring the experience is safe and positive for both of us.

9. How do I get started?

You can visit my websites to learn more about my services, book a session, or schedule a Clarity Call. Whether you're ready to dive in or just curious to learn more, I'm here to support you.

Whether you're exploring this work for the first time or simply seeking to understand yourself better, remember: You're not alone. These services exist because people, just like you, have recognized the value of connection, care, and touch. Taking this step is not just an act of courage—it's an act of self-love.

ABOUT THE AUTHOR

R. Ayité Okyne, *known professionally as Trevor James is a Los Angeles-based men's touch and intimacy coach, massage and cuddle therapist, with many years' experience helping men navigate the complexities of connection, vulnerability, and emotional well-being. With a background that spans living in six countries and a deep curiosity about the human need for touch, Trevor combines his personal journey with professional expertise to create safe, transformative spaces for men to explore intimacy and self-acceptance. His work has empowered countless individuals to embrace their emotional and physical needs, redefining masculinity in a more compassionate and authentic way.*

As a "Third Culture Kid," Ayité brings a unique lens to his work, offering insights into the intersections of culture, identity, and intimacy. His groundbreaking practice has been featured in numerous workshops, retreats, and one-on-one sessions, where he champions the transformative power of touch and emotional presence.

www.ingramcontent.com/pod-product-compliance
Lightning Source LLC
LaVergne TN
LVHW051549070426
835507LV00021B/2488